THE CLIMBING
CHRONICLES

A young climber exploring the mountains of Wales,
the Lake District and Scotland in the 1940s

**bâton
wicks**

For Judith, James and Toni.

THE CLIMBING CHRONICLES

A young climber exploring the mountains of Wales,
the Lake District and Scotland in the 1940s

Harry Parker
Compiled by John Parker

**bâton
wicks**

First published in 2015 by Bâton Wicks.

BÂTON WICKS
Crescent House, 228 Psalter Lane, Sheffield S11 8UT.
www.batonwicks.com

This book is a work of non-fiction based on the diaries of Harry Parker.
The author's estate has stated to the publishers that, except in such minor respects not
affecting the substantial accuracy of the work, the contents of the book are true.

Photography by Harry Parker.

A CIP catalogue record for this book is available from the British Library.

ISBN: 978-1-898573-92-0

Designed and produced by Rod Harrison,
Vertebrate Graphics Ltd. – www.v-graphics.co.uk
Printed and bound in the UK by Berforts Information Press, Stevenage, Hertfordshire.

CONTENTS

HCP outside the Old Dungeon Ghyll Hotel.

Harry Coulston Parker

(1916–1981)

Harry Parker was born in Blackburn on 29 February 1916. He attended Central School, Blackburn and later the Harris College, Preston where he obtained an external degree from London University.

He was employed as a college apprentice by Metropolitan Vickers in Trafford Park before the war, where he became both a chartered electrical and mechanical engineer. He remained with 'Metro Vicks' through the war years until 1960, working as a design engineer and in sales.

At the beginning of 1960 he moved to Bruce Peebles in Edinburgh, returning to Preston in 1962 following his appointment as a lecturer in electrical engineering at the Harris College. He subsequently lectured in Oldham and part time for the Open University following retirement.

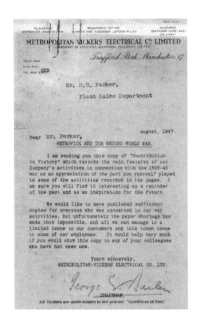

TOP LEFT: LETTER FROM METROPOLITAN VICKERS TO HCP AFTER THE WAR.
TOP RIGHT: HCP – UP NORTH!
BOTTOM: AT METROPOLITAN VICKERS WITH A MOBILE GENERATOR FOR DELIVERY TO THE RAF.

ACKNOWLEDGEMENTS

My father Harry Parker recorded his climbing and mountaineering exploits in detail and we are lucky to have some of his chronicles. I feel that there must have been more but sadly I do not have them.

He started climbing before the war and climbed extensively in the Peak District, editing a guide to the Laddow area in 1948. Notes in his guidebooks also indicate that he was climbing in the Lake District in 1943 (Easter Sunday, Pillar Rock area) and on Skye at Easter 1944.

A large number of his climbing friends and acquaintances worked in Trafford Park, Manchester – one of the largest industrial complexes in the world at that time. Many, including my father, were employed by 'Metro Vicks', which produced massive amounts of military equipment during WW2 including, significantly, the development and production of radar transmitter equipment.

He joined the Karabiner Club in 1945, a year after its formation and subsequently became a member of the Fell and Rock Climbing Club and the Rucksack Club.

I have stayed as close as I could to my father's original text. There was the odd word which, even with my wife's help, I couldn't read and the odd word I didn't understand, so apologies for any spelling mistakes. The language of the day sometimes seems quaint by modern standards but it reflects the period it was written in. Some abbreviations have been written in full for clarity and minor alterations have been made to the text to make it more readable but we have tried to retain the feel of a diary.

Most of the photographs were taken by my father and his friends. I have also included an old Scottish Youth Hostel Association postcard and a photograph taken at Metropolitan Vickers, which no longer now exists.

The excellent book *Unjustifiable Risks* by Simon Thompson provided useful background reading for the period of the *Chronicles*.

Finally a special thank you to Jon Barton and the team at Vertebrate Publishing for their interest and enthusiasm.

John Parker.

ALEX WEIGHING OUT, WINDERMERE.

Our doings
in the Lake District

July 1942

Saturday 11th July

Victoria Station 9.35 by luck and nowt else, everyone seemed to be making tracks for same place. Found couple seats on train in No. 11 platform – fleeting glimpse of Norman & Mother.

Train left 9.50ish stopped Bolton, Chorley and Preston – persuaded nervousy lady not to change – 'crowned' by her suitcase as train jerked into motion. Left Lancaster noon, changed Carnforth – complete with lady and suitcase. Had choc. (wrapped in plain cellophane) on way to Oxenholme – changed again at this fair spot and finally reached Windermere around 1.40.

Weather cloudy (white, low and thick) with intermittent sunshine. Piloted nervousy lady with suitcase into Toby Jug – passable luncheon – jellied veal, salad (ok) bread & butter – cherry flan (excellent), price 3/2 (not so good).

Deposited NL and suitcase at queue for Ambleside bus and returned to weigh rucksack outside Toby Jug.

At the cost of 1d each obtained the following results:
Alex 12 st. 8 lb. without rucksack, 14 st. 10 lb. with 30 lb. rucksack
Self 9 st. 13½ lb.   "   "   "   12 st. 9½ lb.   " 38 lb.   "
Two pairs of boots!

Bought cards and things and sauntered down to Bowness – visited boys and then changed to boots on hill overlooking tennis courts – bar of Alex's chocolate.

Crossed via Bowness ferry in company with hordes of Moira House Schoolgirls and so hit the trail skirting Windermere and going North.

Very warm work in fact almost bloody warm and rather chaffing on the pieds.

Four cyclists only passed us on this stretch. Stopped for sandwiches near Blelham Tarn 5.30 and so to main Ambleside–Skelwith Bridge road.

We were gazing pensively at a Ribble bus timetable when a car came past and stopped down the road. It turned out to be a taxi but the trip in style to Ambleside was under the circumstances cheap at 6d each.

Had a beer each at pub in Waterhead (Waterhead Hotel) and sauntered up towards centre of Ambleside – 1d bus ride to centre – rot setting in and finally caught 7.22 to Grasmere (rather full).

Reached YH just in time for soup course – usual moan from Warden re. lateness (Russian order to be got away!).

Net result of 8- or 9-mile road walk – one blister on sole of left foot and general soreness of both feet – curse it.

After supper dived down to Travellers' Rest but no cider! Had a beer followed by another 'tonic' shandy at the Swan. And the rains came – managed to get our feet wet in dash back through fields.

'It's eleven o'clock British Double Summer Time?'

SUNDAY 12TH JULY

Terrific morning – cloudless etc, repeated last night's performance of cold shower – very acceptable too. Decent brekker – plenty of sugar but surprisingly little milk.

Did my chores i.e. just in time to peel one potato. Warden has a bit of a bark (and large corporation) but runs the place very efficiently and is really quite a good soul.

Took photo of Youth Hostel and sent card to mother.

Left 10ish and proceeded up the valley – took photo of house in foreground and crags at head of valley.

Proceeded to Easedale Tarn non-stop, soles of feet beginning to feel sore and damned hot and rucksack tending to weigh (Alex carrying rope – thank God!).

Carried on to next tarn which proved to be missing – rested and then tackled last bit to col beneath Sergeant Man – sun now gone in but magnificent view. On our way up a bomber had the audacity to fly below the thick white clouds (at about 3,000 ft) and up the Thirlmere Valley below level of Helvellyn.

Skirted back of Pavey Ark and Pikes – feet raising hell at this point! and finally after a last tough bit when rucksack also began to make its presence felt we reached Angle Tarn about 2ish. Here we had lunch with two very cheerful girls Kay (Bournemouth) & Dorothy (Cheltenham) who were going from Elterwater to Wasdale YH in sandals – occasioned by blistered and sore feet. Actually it was their first time in LD but we began to see sense when it transpired that they were just completing training at London College (evacuated to Huddersfield) as gym instructresses for seniors eleven and on.

They had a very amusing way of pinning gaily coloured socks out to dry on back of ruckers.

We carried on together to Esk Hause (photo of Gable in cloud) and Sprinkling Tarn at which point the sun came out, for as it turned out the remainder of the day.

And so to Sty Head and a rest and sunbathe. Here our paths parted and around 4.20 we started along Gable Traverse after taking photos of Piers Ghyll – Scafell on one and Great End on another.

Carefully inspected East Face of Kern Knotts, *Innominate* etc. – photo of *Kern Knotts Chimney* – sky at this time was cloudless and the sunshine and shadows terrific.

We then reached the Needle after a bit of sweat along the Traverse.

Took what should be good photos of Needle and Langmell – Piers Gill (1/125, f11).

Had a 'do' at Wasdale Crack but at the difficult bit thought twice (right foot too shakey after strenuous tramp).

Nice trek along traverse to col between Gable and Kirkfell during which we got a glimpse of IoM and later from the col of Dumfries – photo of panorama.

SCREES FLOWING DOWN TO LINGMELL BECK ON SOUTH SIDE OF GREAT GABLE, AUGUST 1938.

Dropped down in blazing sunshine and rather painfully to Black Sail Hut – noticing on route decent pool for bathing (mental note) – arrived 7.20ish.

Hostel almost full – four girls and ten chaps. Good dinner followed by a bathe and attention to feet. Took view of Hostel in sunshine f11 – 1/25.

Monday 13th July

Bathe in the small pool upstream – good brekker – card to mother. Left Hostel 10 a.m. approx. – down valley through Forestry Commission to bridge over R. Liga, raining very steadily cloud below 2,000 ft.

Climbed up watercourse until we came to what appeared to be base of Pillar – sheltered and had chocolate & cigarette – more climbing damned steep!

Reached a track which appeared too low for High Level Route – crags all round – no sign of Pillar – decided to carry on to top and find ourselves and so arrived on ridge and top of Pillar Mtn. – had lunch 12 a.m.

No sign of Pillar Rock! – took compass bearing and over the edge we go – Pisgah thank goodness – on to the top as a matter of form and then down into Jordan's Gap – still raining.

Examined climbs – crikey are they difficult – look lousy – finally decided to tackle *West Jordan Climb* 50 ft.

Half way up just past the scarp – 'wish I didn't feel so windy' – belayed at top – Alex came up without any trouble. Rambled around top of the rock and then climbed down *Central Jordan*.

Dropped down wicked looking scree to top of this 'ere *Walker's Gully* (Severe).

My hat! – the 'book's' remarks re. the finish of the climb are certainly justified.

Nearly shot down scree and over the top.

Alex climbed up V groove on side of Shamrock and self prospected top of *W. Gully* – def. lousy for a short man.

Decided to give front face of Shamrock a miss due to unhealthy state of 'holds' – lichen covered and very wet!

Finally dropped down to bottom and ate some more chocolate after which carried up hillside track leading to Scarth Gap.

Reached same as we thought 5.10ish (collected horse shoe on top of Scarth Gap) but later on meeting three Yorkshire girls found it to be ten to six and learned they had swiped last of tea at Gatesgarth so we turned round and accompanied them back to base – interesting chat with 'tartan skirt'.

Just in time for supper. After supper Alex & self did a spot of gymnastic work on 'Gable End' and afterwards decided to make a trip with three girls up hillside to rocks at top recommended by Warden as useful for practice.

(L TO R) ALEX, OILY AND TEDDY AT MALHAM TARN, NOVEMBER 1943. ALEX AND OILY MET AT BLACK SAIL HUT.

Alex & Tartan (Oily) reached rocks first and started climbing. Barbara Boat next climbed on left and I stood below giving a running commentary. Dorothy Scaife was just above me when Alex shouts 'look out' and low and behold a large boulder about 2 ft. cube started descending *rapidiment* – at first it seemed to be in my line but suddenly hit the head of a slanting gully and shot in three pieces right at Dorothy. She ducked flat on the floor and the biggest piece passed about a foot or so over her head. Unfortunately there was a certain amount of 'shrapnel' and she was cut on the hand (about ¾ inches and quite deep) and slightly on the face.

We returned with much wisecracking to Hostel, Dorothy fortunately being the nurse of the party did some useful first aid to the accompaniment of Beethoven's *Fifth*.

Had two bars of choc together – Alex mended his boot. I chatted with the Warden (Preston chap) but didn't succeed in getting some tea! – and so to bed, 'The 13th'.

TUESDAY 14TH JULY

Rose 7.30ish cloudy – spot of blue sky – showery. Alex & I had bathe before breakfast.

Peeled spuds as chore. Had word with big Canadian member of RCAF 214 Sq RAF.

Donned shorts and green jersey – packed rucker with rope and horseshoe. Had further words with Oily, Dor & Barb during which promised to respond to request to send prints of Black Sail Hut and one of Napes Needle for Tartan.

After usual farewells left and trudged up Black Sail Pass in dry weather.

Spot of rain near top of pass but that was all.

Chatted to two girls and then started up path to Looking Stead – reached cain below summit and started on High Level Route. Finally reached scree below *Shamrock Traverse* after interesting scramble (no hands!) – had smoke etc. and then climbed to Pillar Rock, establishing base camp near to Pisgah around noon.

Partook of lunch at Filbeck Block during which rain fell and the rock was almost obscured by mist.

Just after lunch mist cleared altogether and rain stopped – valley and far peaks visible.

Started on the job by dropping down to *Old Wall Route* and finding start of *North-East Arête* – (Difficult) – fairly easy climb using hands a lot, up crack to awkward finish involving getting on to sloping ledge – the book's description of this and proceeding ledges as awkward is very apt – finished by way of the incipient chimney at head of *North-East Chimney*. The 'very strenuous pull' can be avoided by a little technique.

And so via top of *Old West Route* to summit.[1]

Considered abseiling down to Jordan Gap but dropped the idea owing to lack of suitable 'hook'.

Climbed down by *Slab and Notch* and so to top of *Walker's Gully*.

Belayed – Alex had look at top of *Walker's Gully* – impressed and then climbed up V chimney as yesterday. Followed him and carried on up face above groove running down face of Shamrock.

Small holds but handholds in right places – new scratch marks – apparently

---

1. Climbs look a bit easier in dry weather but 'damned' exposed. The so-called 'difficults' which abound around the top of the rock, whilst only 5 ft. or so in length, deserve a higher classification on account of said exposure. The book's remarks re. use of rubbers for Severes and above def. apply in this case and serves as pointer to necessity for fine weather! What the hell are we doing here!

blokes we saw earlier when on *NE Arete* have had a 'do' at this part of climb (not named in book and little used by look of things).

Gained top and had Fry's Sandwich.

On cross-over took a view looking down scree to top of *Walker's Gully* with R. Liga in distance.

Dropped down West side of Pisgah and High Man to endeavour to find *West Wall Climb*. 'Crossed the Waterfall' and followed some easy scratch marks to a point which must be start of *WW Climb* since it was about 40 ft. above West Waterfall.

Pitches 1 & 2 few handholds but plenty of friction.

Pitch 3 Pretty straight up – good belay very high up on left between flake and wall – rather tricky changing over to second man.

Pitches 4 & 5 in one. Crack in right wall of 5 pretty good (tackled from left). Climbed second crack to excellent belay. Vertical wall of rain advancing up valley whilst Alex was climbing – 'and the rains came' like stair-rods.

The wall above looked tricky (pitch 6 of *Ledge and Groove*) but the rain washed it out!

Pitch 6 & 7 climbed down crack and delicate balancing movement across ledge under wall to left followed by exposed arm work up arête to belay.

Rain changed to drizzle.

Pitch 8 Worst part getting right foot jammed in smooth groove, rest easy.

And so 'off' by easy scramble to base of High Man and thence to base. Cloud well down – windy and drizzle. Slogged up to top of Pillar Mtn. with rucksacks and so down to 'Windy Gap' – I'll say it was!

Made way slowly down scree to Mosedale and so eventually, notwithstanding bull in field, to Mrs Naylor's.

Four other people staying at farm – two sat down to dinner with us – man and wife originally from Preston, now Chiswick – London.

Dinner excellent – plain but plentiful – soup (kidney), lashings of potatoes, meat & hard beans – followed by terrific suet blackcurrant pudding (9-inch dia.) & tea.

Had queer shandy at Wasdale Head Hotel.

Two single beds in room with H&C, facing Lingmell – accommodation good all round.

WEDNESDAY 15TH JULY

Rose 7.30ish – cold bath and shave (going all pansy).

Weather cloudy – occasional patches of blue. Packed lunches provided look useful.

Left farm after good brekker 10.25 and trudged up valley to foot of Piers Ghyll. Ate bar of choc and gazed with some apprehension at volume of water coming down pitch 1. Stripped to trousers, singlet – waded through water and bridged front of fall. Slight delay whilst Alex passed trilby along rope. Put left foot in crack and looked around for handhold – found something and managed to get weight on left foot. Now close to rock with water cascading off trilby and attempting a spot of 'debagging' – absolutely soaked, continued in towel shirt, jersey and shorts – reached top. Haversack passed up protected by rubber cape. Alex followed quickly and cheated by only getting 30% wet! Scrambled up to pitch 2 'awkward corner' – Alex led by bridging – I followed up face nearer waterfall but we both had to make delicate step across to waterfall head which impressed. And so to a spot of lunch.

Took snap looking up Ghyll and Alex took another of me backing up waterfall.

No trouble on the 40 ft. waterfall pitches, Alex led 15 ft. pitch on right of last waterfall on right-hand side under bridge rock. Much finger tip work – surprised it is not referred to in book since it must be most difficult pitch of climb. Bent edge of nail back on second finger of right hand in the attempt.

Interesting scramble followed to the top – rendered all the more interesting by Alex's antics on rocking stone and subsequently sitting in 3 ft. of water – all square on wetness!

Ghyll ends rather suddenly in scree with waterfall on right – possibilities of 40 ft. pitch climb to right of waterfall.

Made a beeline back to farm and arrived 3.30ish. Hot bath followed by tea with la la lady and then mother and daughter presumably from Wasdale Hall farm who met Freda & Cliff over week-end.

Left farm alone in shorts, rope shoes, jacket, gas cape rolled, 4.40 for Mickledore. Very enjoyable walk up – mist level about 2,000 ft. – passed two climbers and one walker on way finally arriving Mickledore.

Scrambled along *Rakes Progress* and found foot of *Central Buttress* – could only see first pitch (60 ft.) in cloud – looks quite possible. Carried on down to Lord's Rake – had a pipe under rock in Steep Ghyll – examined with morbid interest memorial cross at foot of Pinnacle and so in slight rain back to farm for 7.40.[2] Very Nice!

Oldish lady (school teacher type) and young 'un' staying night at farm – presumably live at Ambleside (evac. from London probably).

Bottle of Bass at Wasdale which possibly was responsible for terrific bowel movement prior to going to bed. Rain started coming down in real Lakeland style about 9 p.m. and continued throughout night.

---

2. 1903 memorial to four climbers who died on *Pinnacle Face* on Scafell.

THURSDAY 16TH JULY

Rain still descending, mist and cloud lowest I have ever seen – level about 50 ft. above valley – lifted later in morning.

Spent morning alternately chatting to two women from Ambleside (teachers) and writing cards to people:

Letter cards – Will, mother, Madge, Totty.
Card Wasdale Head, Ada G.
Composite views of Wasdale Head, Denis D.

Made some tea and four of us had our sandwiches – unfortunately had to keep turning walkers away.

Left for Sty Head 1.40 in dry weather – other two going over Black Sail. Just prior to making top rain came down at rare pace – 'sheltered' near stone until three girls came along asking nearest way to Gillerthwaite. Decided to take them along *Gable Traverse*. Had bar of choc and took over two rucksacks at *Kern Knotts Crack* and so slowly to col between Gable and Kirkfell – intermittent rain and wind.

Left girls to carry on after more choc and returned high up across White Napes, Little Hell Gate under Sphinx Rock to Dress Circle – rain completely stopped and cloud level above us.

Napes Needle: Rock still wet – climbed up *Wasdale Crack* – had a struggle at narrow bit halfway up owing to wetness and so to the shoulder – bumped my left elbow in the process – blood all over. Alex followed with little trouble and belayed onto Mantleshelf.

Attained the Mantleself with ease and edged round left corner – paused to allow wind to drop – after examination decided to get both feet on corner and so vertically up the sloping face – belayed. Alex reached top after a little trouble and then quickly descended – I followed using rope slung round top. Had a little difficulty in twitching rope off rock.

Descended *Crack* and found the narrow bit quite easy compared to ascent.

Afterwards 'ran' up *Needle Ridge* and found it a cinch – very windy. Came down *Lit. Hell Gate* – collected capes and so down scree to Styhead Pass – Alex a little bad tempered at this point – feeling peckish, cold and fed up I suppose.

Reached farm 8 p.m. in time for supper with Stanley Thompson – Margaret (his attachment) and two Prestonites.

Very interesting chat with Thompson 'altered shape of *Napes Needle* by levering four blocks off Shoulder necessitating change to Fell & Rock Club badge!' – hence he hasn't got one.

At present in Workington – spent short time in Manchester during which met Stan Mullins of Laddow fame.

Had hottish bath and then a Bass at hotel – gassy! Made entry in Climbing Book re. Napes Needle and Napes Ridge.

FRIDAY 17TH JULY

Wakened early – felt a bit off – stomach probably caught chill yesterday and Bass too gassy and bad.

Raining on and off most of morning – cloud about 1,500 ft.

Wrote and sent cards to:
Kern Knotts – Mrs & Miss Mitchell
Wasdale Hotel – Mother & Mr Neville

Lounged about until Stan Thompson & Margaret Young left to go to Styhead. Went to bed until lunch time 12.30.

Lunched off tomatoes, lettuce, cheese, bread & butter, tea & cakes.

Left 2 p.m. in dry weather – sauntered up to Hollow Stones and thence to foot of Moss Ghyll. Scafell very wet with the Ghyll even wetter.

First pitch very slimy – interesting doing chockstones without using one's back.

Second pitch useful variation on *W. Wall* 6 ft. to left of chimney – climb about 10 ft. vertical and then step on to ledge – delicate movement round corner and step across to head of chimney.

Pitch 3 climbed on slab to right – too wet in chimney – half way up pitch there was an interesting thing, climb across slabs to chockstone at head of chimney – we didn't do this.

7 & 8 Tennis Court Wall – interesting – probably only difficult part of climb – rather exposed and delicate traverse round to scree below cave.

10 Boltie Step delicate but easy with trics.

Came out of the amphitheatre by Boltie Exit to top of *Pisgah* – very windy but dry – good view North – Dumfries just discernible under cloud ceiling. Bar of choc and so down Broad Stand to Mickledore and *Rakes Progress*. Examined Flake portion of *Central Buttress* from *Progress* – there seems to be a sling left in convenient position.

Gathered later that the worst isn't over on passing Flake, pitches 10 & 11 very delicate traverses.

Alex reached farm 6.50 and self 7.15 – rain and sunshine on way down – Shamrock, Scafell Pike and waterfall looked good in sunshine.

People from hut just leaving farm when I arrived. Haydal 'what mystifies me is, how you get inside that coil of rope' – 'Grew up inside from a child'.

Went round with Stan & Marg to Brackenclose. Gang of five were at farm making supper. A. B. Hargreaves also around.

Vic showed us some interesting tricks afterwards – rope balancing – tree traverse and board and roller.

Miss Winck rather a curiosity – terrific front top teeth and fond of introducing the Dolomites.

Saturday 18th July

Out of bed about 7 a.m. – clouds about 2,500 ft. – occasional rain.

Had brekker 8 a.m. – bacon & eggs, lashings of butter, bread, marmalade & honey. Paid Mrs Naylor £2 each – Stan & Marg and married couple down for brekker as we left 9.30.

Posted card to mother. Stomach belchy and bowels still bound but signs of freeing.

Slogged up Sty Head Pass and thence to Kern Knotts.

Put back bar of choc – changed to climbing boots and roped up for *Kern Knotts Crack*.

Pitch 1 reached Sentry Box easily by which time Stan, Marg & father had arrived – afraid I indulged in spot of free swearing unthinkingly.

Stan gave me instruction re. climb to right of crack – ok but rock rather wet in vital spot so after they pushed on decided to sweat up crack.

Using Alex's shoulder indulged in a spot of real work and so to the top – belayed and gave Alex a turn at working.

Abseiled down to Sentry Box and on rope did move on right *à la* Thompson with slight variation – right foot in T position and right hand moved to V crack above – left finger taken out of hole and then leaned across to put palm of hand on opposite sharp edge of crack followed by left boot –

with three-pt. support brought right hand to horizontal edge on right hand side of crack – edged up and brought left hand to same position but better hold – muscled up.

Went down again and repeated with slack rope – very neat and easy after first go.

Dropped to bottom and then climbed *Inominate* on rope in boots – a cinch fairish of handholds but a certain amount of balancing required.

Alex then attempted spot of sheep rustling but sheep had other ideas and jumped to another crag so we left it. Slogged up track and reached Esk Hause 2 p.m. – weather quite dry but no sun. Two Scotties just finishing lunch – students Glasgow University – very nice chaps (one engineering t'other chem.) – using Primus gave us cup of soup followed by coffee & cigarettes – on way to Black Sail.

Left them 2.50 and after much scrambling and bilberry picking reached foot of NW face of Gimmer and located *Asterisk Route* – sun started shining at this point – thank goodness!

Photo of *Asterisk* from above jammed block. Started *Asterisk* in boots – sunny and calm.

Pitch 1 very nice – sharp belay.

Pitch 2 – easy – decent belay. Rock slopes away at nice angle – rough and dry.

Pitch 3 – start easy but gaining of ledge tricky and traverse to ridge delicate. Stance on edge of ridge BA and belay not as good as FRCC guide would have us believe!

Change over damned awkward – last pitch 45 ft. first half using diagonal crack to left for handholds fairly easy – decent handholds petered out 6 ft. from top – stuck – went back to small ledge – returned a little higher well spreadeagled – hands began to give and feet tremble a little, decided had to make a 'do' of it and did! Somehow got one hand over lip of rock and just hung there thankful. 'Most heroic thing I've ever done in my life.'

Alex followed by yet another route – on inspection found that I should have gone further to left – three decent handholds in a row not visible from below. Heard during climb, 'I would risk my life on these trics'.

Photos: top of *Asterisk*, down gully from jammed block and Alex, another of *Asterisk*.

Reached Grisedales' Farm 7.45, photo of Alex & self in battle dress. Alex had beer and self shandy in Old Dungeon Ghyll. Reached Langdale Hotel 9 p.m. – further drinks! and so to Youth Hostel and supper after spot of kidding.

SUNDAY 19TH JULY 1942

Very sunny morning – took photo of Youth Hostel. Left rucks at YH and sauntered up High Close, photo of Pikes and so on to ridge (photo of Helvellyn). Left Alex and walked over to crags below Silver Howe, photos of Pikes, Bowfell etc.

Met Alex at Langdale – tea at Brittania and so on 1.10 bus to Ambleside and thence to Windermere by 1.50. Lunch and tea at Elleray Hotel, two photos of Windermere Lake thro' trees and one of Alex on weighing machine.

Journey back on 5.45 train uneventful – changed Preston arrived Victoria 9.40 and digs 10.30 – pretty packed between Oxenholme and Carnforth. 'Plenty of room near ceiling unused yet.'

HCP TACKLES AMEN CORNER.

LANGDALE

1942

WEDNESDAY 23RD SEPTEMBER

Rose at the unearthly hour of 5.30 a.m. – raining and dark – Mother prepared light breakfast – not feeling like anything ambitious – stomach off, bilious.

Left 6 East Lancashire Rd. 6.35 – rain stopped and cycled to town – rucksack damned heavy!

Single to Windermere for self 9/6 – cycle 2/9. Left on 7.03 to Preston – train rather full of work people no trouble with cycle in guard's van.

Train from Preston 8.12 presumably starts from there and goes with five stops to Kendal.

Old Johnny in comp. started to argue about religion but the other reg. travelers weren't having any – he was shut up – apparently none too popular with two ladies present judging from the way they ripped into him. Had comp. to self from Lancaster.

Arrived Kendal 9.50 decided to cycle remainder – rained (sleet) twice on way. Bought views in Windermere and Ambleside and finally reached Langdale Estate in thoroughly exhausted (lack of food I expect and biliousness) condition 12.30ish.

Bob in common room of Wayfarer Lodge.[1]

---

1. Bob Whyte: colleague at 'Metro Vicks'.

Consumed an excellent lunch and so cycled up the valley to Old Dungeon Ghyll Hotel.

Spot of rain on the way, climbed *Middlefell* – usual struggle on first pitch – not feeling too clever.

Second real pitch tried variation on left over overhang (on rope) down and up seemed reasonable.

Had a shot at left hand side (direct) but gave it up as rain and sleet descended.

Carried on to Gimmer in slight rain – short snack and reconnoitered Bilberry Chute – Ash Tree Ledge etc.

Tried traverse to Amen Corner but Bob wouldn't follow – too wet.

Decided to make back for Old Dungeon – which did by long way round along valley bottom. Drank a pint shandy and so, after attempt on problem rock, to Langdale. Cloud burst during last mile wet me through.

THURSDAY 24TH SEPTEMBER 1942

Brekker 9 a.m. after which cycled up the valley to Grisedales' farm – one or two showers on way. Went up *Middlefell* (except first pitch – three climbers thereon) – did variation on second pitch without rope – ok and so to Gimmer.

Short snack and then tackled *Bracket and Slab*. Bob in rubbers (very ancient) and self in boots.

Lovely traverse diag. to left just below bracket – bracket awkward for self but easy for Bob (question of reach) followed by airy balancy movement up a crack (end of pitch 3).

The Neat Bit interesting and so to the Gangway. The Chimney was very wet and after an attempt decided that the struggle wasn't worth it. 'This pitch is very hard, very strenuous, and usually also very wet' I'll say! So climbed chimney on *Gimmer Chimney* climb. Beautiful balance traverse (horizontal) on slabs at top.

Descended *South-East Gully* and partook of another snack.

Changed to rubbers and found start of *'B' Route* on Ash Tree Ledge.

First scramble easy and so up an interesting variation to left of pitch 2 – balancy but lovely handhold at top.

Amen Corner is a layback and overhangs – damned hard work.

And so up the Gallery to foot of Green Chimney – starts to rain so removed rubbers and climb in stocking feet – rather *exposé* and hard to feet! Reached apparently Crow's Nest and so up fairly easy slabs (once again in stockinged feet) to top – brought Bob up and donned rubbers.

Decided after *Kern Knotts Crack* not to do any more of these strenuous pitches where one sweats and sweats and gets no place.

Descended *South-East Gully* to Langdale track at foot of *B&S* – slight drizzle.

Went halfway along traverse to Amen Corner but too much water dripping down and Bob reluctant to follow so returned.

Weather cleared up and so got down to Old Dungeon around 5ish. Partook of excellent tea (for the times) 1/9 and got into conversation with one of three members of Alpine Club we bypassed on *Middlefell* earlier in day. Through Bob arranged to lead three of them on Gimmer the following day Friday.

Magnificent evening after tea – cycled slowly back – had a 'do' at 'split rock' but arms too tired.

Bathed before dinner – lit fire in common room – later sauntered round to Langdales for shandy – perfect evening – full moon and all that.

Returned to WL and chatted with two girls in common room.

Retired 11ish, sent cards to mother, Alex, Ada, Barbara (Lupes Needle) and Dave Adshead. Mr Neville on Friday.

FRIDAY 25TH SEPTEMBER

Fine morning – cloudy, Bob rose early – had brekker 7.30 and left to cycle to Windermere for 9.25 a.m. train.

Left Langdale Estate 10ish and cycled up valley taking two shots of Pikes on the way.

Two members of party sat on pebbles in sun. Mears (Engineer – short and wiry) and Grosvenor (tall and rather distinguished looking) – should say both in the region of sixty.

Booth the bloke we spoke to came out shortly afterwards (average size, forty odd, wearing glasses – rather 'cowish' expression)

We trudged by short track to foot of Gimmer – Booth supplying us with Barley sugars on way to keep up our strength.

During our walk learned that Warren (dist. feature, green Grenfell trousers) was ahead – apparently on the last Everest 'do' in 1938, I suppose.[2]

Had words with him re. climbs – typical 'Englishman abroad' type – horsey moustache about thirty and little over average build.

We then assembled on Ash Tree Ledge – found the start of *Oliverson's Variation* and donned our rubbers.

---

2. Charles Warren, Cambridge-educated doctor who was a member of the 1935, 1936 and 1938 Everest expeditions.

Booth tied on second, Grosvenor third and Mears fourth.

First pitch easy scramble – brought Booth & Gros. up. Subsequent attempts at belaying by Booth revealed either that he hadn't much idea (notwithstanding his statement re. climbs done with Selincourt in '24) or was just careless.

Shall have to climb as if there were no second, I suppose.

Rather delicate traverse to right and then up awkward crack to middle of Forty Foot Corner. (Now on 'A' Route)

After being given more rope carried on to top of FF Corner and belayed on good spike.

And so round to left up Lichen Chimney and final crack on 'A' Route to top of Crag.

Down SE Gulley and so to lunch on Ash Tree Ledge.

Whilst we ate sandwiches two people were on OV – Dankin (Sec. of Alpine and Climbers' Clubs) round corner on Forty Foot and the strangest of apparitions smoking his pipe patiently at top of first pitch.

Surely it could be the original member of the Alpine Club – anyway he looked like such – age sixtyish – drooping Walrus moustache – thin features – old drooping pipe – very old and battered brown Trilby – (very) old jacket with patches and ye gods! the original stove pipe trousers – shame though – he is climbing in rubbers!

We then found start of 'B' Route near cairn and soon disposed of first easy scramble.

As a variation took them up vertical wall to left of second pitch on 'B' Route – little or no difficulty. Traversed along ledge and round corner to foot of Amen Corner.

After sorting rope out, against my wishes I had to go first – so that Gros. took a photo of me on the Corner instead of I taking one of them as intended.

Usual strenuous struggle – Booth failed twice (arms giving out) so sent him round to right (on *B&S* climb).

Grosvenor followed ok remarking at the top that he wouldn't expect many grandfathers to have climbed that bit. Crikey – I'll say.

Mears followed, perhaps not quite as 'clean' as Gros!

Up the Gallery across foot of Green Chimney – traverse round corner and then up delightfully exposed face to the Cave – broke the pitch by traversing to left to belay at top of Lichen Chimney.

Brought up Booth & Gros. Returned to Cave and then continued vertically upwards of continuous severity *all* the way up – I agree. Plenty of handholds though, if thin but gloriously exposed. The Alpine Club laddies enjoyed it.

When we returned to Ash Tree Ledge, Warren and second were halfway up '*D' Route*, Considered following them alone but invited to go down to Old Dungeon for tea – Which did.

During afternoon heard motorbike noises coming from Gable direction and later a Blenheim or somesuch flew up the valley and out over Stake Pass. We later learned that eight motor cyclists had gone over Stake Pass – good luck to them!

Enjoyed my tea – met Mear's wife – fairly interesting conversation (from NZ to Chamonix – good for rock work).

Gros. has daughter Mary (married I suppose) who I notice in F&R Club *Journal* 1936-37 was with her father at Alpine meet Montenvers (Chamonix) in 1936.

As we moved out to lounge prepared to leave and was 'seen off' at the gate.

Water lovely and hot – had bath – dined with others in Pillar Hotel (food not as good as Gateway) and then dashed off with two ladies to a lecture dealing with US. Very good speaker M. A. from Keswick (Jones) never stopped. Inclined to be a little off the mark in engineering refs but otherwise good.

Three visitors – oldish man, Edith & I only ones to ask questions. Finished at 9.30.

SATURDAY 26TH SEPTEMBER

Tied rope to bars and donned boots in an attempt at relieving my seat of too much adhesion to cycle saddle.

Left about 10 a.m. in excellent weather – blue cloudless sky. Uneventful run to Kendal and then the fun began – short spin to Sedbergh involving 800 or so foot climb up hill similar to Shear Brow![3] – Lovely drop into Sedbergh for 1.15 p.m. – lunched at CTC in main street which incidentally lined with books (1 mile of books effort) – lunch a swindle at 3/6.

Cycled and walked up Garsdale stopping for 15 mins. to repair puncture and so to Garsdale Head where I picked up a puppy spaniel (made the mistake of patting the thing) – feeling rotten at the time – cramp on stomach – easily winded – nearly put myself out tearing down hills in an endeavor to shake off my pup – pup full of energy and truly great sight when loping alongside at speed. Finally shook him off in the run down to Hawes.

Reached same about 4.15 p.m. and partook of cup of tea. Saw more tanks in this Dales village than any other time or place during the war.

Another slog up hillside to Wether Fell – arms tired and feeling the effect of pushing cycle over 1,000 ft. climb!

3. Shear Brow: notoriously steep hill in Blackburn.

Exhilarating drop down into Langstrothdale Chase – and much appreciated the greenness and generally fresh appearance of the dale after the wild outlook of the moors.

And so to Buckden for 7 p.m. and a plain but excellent tea at CTC place. – interesting conversation with couple of Settle-ites. Found out that time was pretty limited if Hellifield to be reached for train at 9.20 or so.

Shot down to Kettlewell and Kilnsey where I forked West and found start of track across moors to Malham – at foot of 600 or so foot climb – confirmed by cyclist who had just come over from Malham – told me it was 7.45 and it had taken him 1¾ hrs. from *Malham* – ye gods I have 1½ hrs. to get to Hellifield.

The ensuing ¼ hrs. or so climb on to Malham moor must be toughest ever experienced – cycle felt heavy – pushing against time, breath coming in very short pants and sweating cobs – could have sat down and wept.

Finally made it – feeling much better – stomach ok.

Fortunately twin walls guided me across moor – still dark – moon not risen.

Cycled as fast as dared – a real gamble – fortunately no boulders in the way.

By a piece of excellent navigation found fork left and finally came (with a sigh of relief) on to metalled road.

Started dropping down Gardale Scar – road getting steeper and steeper until I thought I was going to loop the loop.

Shot through Malham (incidentally faint outline of surrounding crags suggests a future visit not to be sneezed at) to the strains of final part of Music Hall (finish 9 p.m.).

By another even greater example of excellent navigation negotiated turns and crossroads betwixt Malham and Hellifield finally shot up on to the platform of Hellifield station only to have the news broken to me gently that it was 9.15 and the train left at 9.10 (i.e. last train). Another 20 miles to cycle! Decided to have a drink before starting so repaired to only decent (quite good) pub Hellifield possesses.

Staggered into pukka lounge (adorned with two or three bright young things) and ordered firmly small whisky & pint of beer only to be told 'we don't serve pints in the lounge'. 'What do you serve' says I. 'Oh you can have two gills' says she.[4] Ok gimme – ye gods!

Removed the 'sma' from sight quickly and then sat back to appreciate the two gills and a cigarette – not giving a damn about the curious glances of the locals.

Left about 9.30 p.m. – moon now shining and run quite pleasant – uneventful except for stop by constable at foot of Sawley Brow for being without light ('accidental I assure you' – switched on again).

Stopped at Billington to finish off remaining sandwiches – feeling tired now – evening cold but moon excellent.

Reached home about 11.30 after being nearly finished off by incline from tram terminus.

Mother waiting for me – really enjoyed the subsequent meal.

Trip in all took 13½ hrs. for 90 or so miles and 2,000 ft. of climbing – fortunately no rain all day.

Except for tiredness finished feeling fine – stomach ok.

Must return to the Dales some time – especially Malham and district.

---

4. A 'gill' was local slang for half a pint.

HCP ᴏᴜᴛsɪᴅᴇ Pᴇɴ-ʏ-Pᴀss.

CHRISTMAS IN SNOWDONIA

1942

THURSDAY 24TH DECEMBER

Left Metro Vicks 4 p.m. – Exchange about 4.17 – booked to Llandudno Jnct. return for each of us (Alan, Alex & self) and cycles – 19/8 each.[1]

Train rather full so got in luggage van at front of train – well filled with people – we sitting in the balcony – train left to time 4.30 p.m., non-stop to Warrington where more people crowded in. Had our first snack and so slowly to Chester about 6 p.m. – followed by another snack, 'shall we throw a few crumbs down to the mob below' says Alan.

Non-stop to Prestatyn followed by a third snack and chocolate. Incidentally saw 'Bill the Babfiter' at Exchange – he left us at Chester – going walking apparently.

Reached Ll. Jnct. about 7.40 and changed for Bangor – thought advisable in view of drizzle – 30-mile ride none too attractive!

Again in the luggage van but now with talkative trio, one of which we had met at Laddow and Castle Naze – one Dennis Oliver complete with ex-'Pat Kelly's husband' ice axe – 2⅜-inch blade, 4 inches long – 6-inch pick about ⅝ inches deep with serrations on underside about 1 inch from end – total length of axe 34 inches approx. – just my weight – side members

---

1. Alan Veale and Alec Chisholm – friends from 'Metro Vicks'. Alan would later become managing director of GEC Power Engineering and Alec professor of mechanical engineering at the University of Salford.

part of head riveted to shaft – oval 1⅜-inch major axis.[2]

Shot off their mouths all way to Bangor. Here we parted with Alex and caught train to Bethesda which reached about 8.40 – where we walked off the station in usual casual manner without paying excess fare.

After brief passage of arms with local policeman over shining light on pub sign finally found ourselves in another pub for a ½-pint of nut brown.[3]

Spot of singing accompanied by accordion well under way but nipped in the bud by our friendly sergeant – the locals seem to knuckle under easily. Only comment 'I supply him with coal but I'll see he doesn't get any next week.'

And so on our way up the Pass – first mile rather bloody but after that all well – arrived Ogwen Cott. 10ish. Partook of decent supper of baked beans on toast, bread, butter & jam, tea & sugar.

FRIDAY 25TH DECEMBER

Asked to be called for 8.15 but actually about 8.50 – Ogwen time different to ours!

Finally left 10.30 a.m. after receiving advice on how to find *Gt. Gully* from Ffynnon (salts or something).

Weather fine but cloudy – cycled up to eleventh milestone and then up track on left to farm on hillside (Glan Llugwy) where bikes were left. Skirted Ffynnon Llugwy on East bank to North-E. corner in cloud and so up to the Shoulder and down t'other side. After a few bosh shots found the Amphitheatre and Buttress but couldn't make up our minds which was the *second* gully. Had lunch in what looked like the second *real* gully.

---

2. Pat Kelly founded the Pinnacle Club for women climbers in 1922. Her husband Harry Kelly was a leading figure of Lakeland climbing between the wars.

3. The war-time blackout was in force at this time.

Actually climbed to the right of real gully and found ourselves in a hell of a mess to the right of terrific overhanging slab which dripped oodles of water – attempted chimney but decided too tough under conditions (no nail marks anyway).

Climbed up gully in which we had lunch and found it to open out on to hillside at Western extremity of rocks. Incidentally many bits of aeroplane down this gully incl. duralumin rudder support – apparently seven planes distributed over the Carnedds!

And so to the top. Quickly found the *top* of *Great Gully* – recognisable by well-worn nature of top of large jammed boulder – also small wall built across gully.

Decided to climb down – *First Pitch* very interesting – ledge leading inside large cave followed by step down edge of large chockstone and complicated move to get under same (extraction of one's finger from crack rather painful!)

The only real pitch occurred about halfway down and called *Great Chimney*. I first of all bypassed it on right side with Alan belayed above and then climbed chimney (about 40 ft) first on right then backing up slightly to lowest of three chockstones on left where a cross-over was made. Continued up the left edge until a slight overhang was reached at the top necessitating a delicate step over with right foot to the right wall and a lean forward to grasp a small flake. All one's weight is then taken on one's arms and balance shifted over on to right leg. The move from this position across a little slab necessitates a tricky piece of balancing work – ve-ery strenuous.

Alan then went down on rope without any difficulty but I after fiddling about on the slab couldn't just face the placing of my security on my arms so decided to take the by-passing route.

The rest of the climb consisted of scrambling pitches and vertical waterfall pitches without any technical difficulty.

Touched down in about 2 hrs. – climb supposed to be 600 ft.

Returned to summit and rewarded by glorious views of sinking sun – occasional white clouds and red glow in the East.

Incidentally we had occasional glimpses of a fine day and sunlight landscape in descending *Gt. Gully* but as usual in such things it was *wet* and dark. So that as usual and notwithstanding the dry day we came out pretty soaked.

Reached farm and collected bikes about 6 p.m. and so to Ogwen in good time to change for Christmas dinner.

Eleven of us sat down for dinner – four new arrivals and one with a woolly jacket apparently worn inside out for inside wear to show the wool! Dinner excellent pork chops – carrots (lashings of), potatoes, apple sauce, stuffing, Christmas pud – in flames (meths or paraffin used – surely not alcohol – although could taste nothing but pud). Followed by mince pies & tea – not bad.

During all this it transpired that the other five lads led by Ffynnon were going to paint out the V at top of Milestones with green paint later on in the evening. We were invited to join in the expedition.

Paid a visit to Idwal Cot. and found Dennis Oliver and Co having supper (9 p.m.) and rest of hostellers 'reeling' etc.

Duly admired almost completed mural decorations of local scenes in dining room – much amusing by bloke fallen out of picture and pair of feet in top bunk.

Impressed Oliver by shooting a line about Milestone Buttress in darkness and *Munich Climb*.

Blokes making prep. at Ogwen – announced our intention of climbing *Milestone Direct* in moonlight and arranged to meet at top. Found foot of climb and Buttress in shadows of mountain with two blokes fiddling about.

Climbed up 100 or so feet finding it rather awkward having to feel nature of each foothold and handhold – Alan followed quickly.

Next pitch leading up to hard traverse to garden wall set a standard of technique by stepping on one finger with a tricouni – what comes of combining hand- and foot-holds! A hallmark of climbing skill will therefore be a tric mark on one or more fingers!

Reached top, after slight struggle up chimney, about midnight – no painters present – went down on a rope to inspect the V – still there so repaired to base and bed for 1.30 a.m. – painters still out stooging around somewhere.

Other crazy 'goings on' included a bunch of hostellers who seemed intent on bathing in the lake at one o'clock in the morning and a couple of blokes 'sleeping' on top of Tryfan between Adam & Eve stones.

Learned the morning after that the V was duly painted out and party returned 3 a.m.

SATURDAY 26TH DECEMBER

Called 7.40 for breakfast at 8 a.m. which was as good as usual. Weather fine and clear but cloud gathering in the east.

Left on cycles 9.10 a.m. for Capel and Pen-y-Pass passing Dyffryn on the way – time of the day with 'John Davies' & 'Thomas' – cloud low in Snowdon direction.

And so up slog from Pen-y-Gwryd hotel to Pen-y-Pass – reached Gorphwysfa hotel for 10.15 – no Alex in view – arrived with Dorothea about 10.30.[4]

Adjourned to hotel for tea followed by abandoned efforts of Alex at taking our photographs.

4. Gorphwysfa hotel apparently the place to stay for climbing on Lliwedd – Climbers' Club centre – looks attractive – slightly Swiss.

Parted at 11 a.m. Alex & Dorothea taking PYG track for the Horseshoe and we the Miners' Track.

Skirted South-East bank of Llyn Llydaw and then up hillside – scree a helluva length – not surprising when we came out on top having missed the cliffs through being too near Snowdon, we thought – very difficult in mist without a compass.

Had luncheon top and descended working east – finally decided that cliffs weren't high enough and we were in wrong place i.e. too far *from Snowdon* so back we went and found the real cliffs (still in mist) and also realized we had missed the blasted things by a few yards in our upward 'slog'.

The mist or cloud decided to rise at this juncture.

Y Lliwedd is a rare cliff – very exposed – firmer in appearance than one might expect and with a marvelous view across Llydaw and the Glyders.

Stooged around in *Central Gully* – very wet but very interesting – all the VS climbs at this point – of short length but high up on the cliff starting from a sort of amphitheatre, *Swastika* too looked very interesting.

Reached the top by our scree – had a few sandwiches and left 4.05 to start the Horseshoe – met Alex & Dorothea shortly afterwards who seemed rather aghast at our idea of starting at that time.

Trod on it – helluva sweat up 600 or so feet to Snowdon summit – steepest bit of path I know of? – worse than Gable! – summit 'made' for 4.50. Signs of Radiolocation work in progress – large telegraph pole at highest point with two dipoles.

Thick cloud – shot off down to Crib-y-Ddysgl and so along ridge with a cold wet wind on our right flank – made Crib Goch peak at end of ridge for 6.05 and darkness.

Tricky dropping down face of Crib Goch but helped by wind as a direction indicator and occasional glimpses of scratched rock. Finally made PYG track but later lost it again in dark, getting too low down on hillside and involved with many stones, boulders and barbed wire entanglements.

After a tussle with a sheep pen (disused – very) found the PYG and so to the hotel for 7.05 p.m.

Alex & Dorothea were awaiting us not worrying unduly consoling themselves with beer & tea – arrived there about 6 p.m.

Alan & I had a quick Bass and then the convoy started for Fachwen.

Our objective was reached after a brief stop in Llanberis for purchase of cigarettes.

Last hill up to the cottage very tiring – this child completely overcome!

Kath & John waiting for us with plenty of good things ready.

Deposited most of wet things in glory hole followed by wash and excellent dinner enlivened with anecdotes from Kath & John and ourselves.

Prior to this the goat was duly inspected but she after inspecting us showed her contempt in a marked manner.

Kath & John had had a struggle with the cottage – 35 lbs. of paint used to overcome black outlook of dining room with great success – two more bedrooms – kitchen and glory hole all on ground floor – attic but no water laid on – all for 2/8 per week!

After a very pleasant few hours left just before midnight cycling via Pentir and Bethesda to Ogwen. Weather very threatening but grand – except for steep hill in first mile cycled all way from Bethesda to Ogwen – a truly stout effort in our condition.

Arrived Ogwen 1.30ish.

SUNDAY 27TH DECEMBER

Rose 8.45 – weather fine but cloud rather low – breakfasted eventually alone other lazy so and so in bed.

Left cottage about 10.25 on cycles – deposited same at tenth milestone – V still green!

Slogged up to Heather Terrace and finally found *South Gully* fairly easily – top of Tryfan in cloud – sat down for lunch opposite Gashed Crag.

Started climbing same 12.05 – first 100 feet to scrambly bit a cinch and so to pitch leading up to the Gash, decided to take V groove next to *South Gully* – untrodden apparently by the feet of man.

Handholds few and thin, all depended on foot – groove fell away unrestricted to Gully – half way up next move very uncertain – legs a bit shaky after exertions of past few days – fought a very interesting battle with myself before we could agree to make the next rather risky move – but finally got my right hand on flakey handhold on top right of groove – phew!

Alan followed easily and we belayed at foot of very well worn chimney – rest of climb uneventful except for bit lacking satisfying handholds at top of slab.

Gained top of Tryfan between 2 and 2.30 and partook of sandwiches.

Views in direction of Anglesey superb – sea visible – curious effect of cloud gathering on east side of Tryfan but absolutely clear on West side. Probably due to wind blowing from West.

Left summit about 2.30 and decided to have a shot at record from top to road. Found it warm work descending – legs not quite as steady as would like – after scrambling down initial rocky portion took scree on left and made a beeline for road striking path leading to road at spot a little nearer Idwal than tenth milestone. Time taken 15 mins. as against known record of 13 mins. Alan found descending grassy slopes minus heels not so good and decided to take 19 mins.

Dripping with perspiration cycled back to Ogwen Cot.

During our tea there various objects came for sustenance including one carrying a 'tall shiner'. Apparently he carried this thing around (or wore same) on his expeditions judging by his remark that the thing occasionally became jammed in chimneys. I gather he is portrayed on Idwal Cottage mural decorations.

Paid bill – 33/- each plus 2/- for Gwen.

Left OC 4 p.m. and cycled at great velocity down to Bangor taking about 30 mins.

Alan bought tickets 2/5 single to Ll. Jn. plus 11d for cycle which we didn't really require to buy.

Alex awaiting us on station – partook of cup of tea giving Alan some so that he could return the cups and get ticked off for bringing same out of refreshment room.

Put bikes in lug. van at front and found plenty of room in compartment nearby.

5 p.m. train left 5.20 (from Holyhead) and after rather dreary journey reached Eccles 10.30 and so on our cycles to our respective digs.

THE KARABINER CLUB WAS FORMED IN 1944, BY A GROUP OF YOUNG CLIMBERS WITH
NEW IDEAS, AS AN ALTERNATIVE TO THE ESTABLISHED CLUBS. THE NAME WAS EVEN A SNUB
TO THE OLDER GENERATION WHO CONSIDERED KARABINERS TO BE A MECHANICAL DEVICE
AND TOTALLY UNACCEPTABLE.

SIGNATURES ON THE PHOTOGRAPH: FOUNDER MEMBERS: PLUM AND ROBBIE WORRALL,
LEONARD STUBBS, CLIFFORD WOOD, ERIC FLITCROFT (HON SEC). PRESIDENT: J. E. BYROM
(1950-1953). OTHER MEMBERS: GEOFFREY HALLAWELL (1945), C GRIFFITHS (1946),
JOAN WILLIAMS, DESMOND STEVENS.

GLENCOE EXPEDITION

EASTER 1945

THURSDAY 29TH MARCH

Granted afternoon off to attend Alex's wedding[1] (very convenient!) and therefore left the Works 12 noon for Alex's flat. Posted letter to Mother on the way and arrived 12.30 p.m. – Alex in residence, Oily, Ken, Alan, Barbara & 'Corky' putting in an appearance.

Partook of 'wedding breakfast' after presenting on behalf of the ECC the *Skye Chronicles* (Easter 1944). The splendid wedding cake was duly cut by Alex's ice axe and was part consumed, tasted marvelous.

All gang then trooped by bus to the Altrincham Registery where Henshie was awaiting us. Oily & Alex were fixed in about 15 mins. (2.20) for the sum of £2-13-1d- this gave rise to the usual engineering wisecracks about the high piece work prices! (Barbara & Ken witnesses.)

After the ceremony the party re-bussed back to the flat for a drink and odd speech or two. Alan, Henshie & I were then fortunate to catch a 48 bus to town and we arrived Exchange 8 mins. to 4 for the 4.03 train to Glasgow.

There was a queue at the booking office so to save time we booked Glasgow returns – £2-5-7d.

Dashed on to the platform 4.01 p.m. only to find the train packed from

---

1. Alex and Aline (Oily) first met at Black Sail hut July 1942.

end to end including all baggage vans except the end coach. Tried unsuccessfully to effect an entry but the guard was adamant – so the train left us on the platform!

A station policeman tipped us off that the 4.25 from Platform 12 connected the 4.03 we had missed at Preston (the train actually bound for that popular resort, Blackpool). Said train was boarded and we arrived in Preston to find half of the 4.03 waiting for us – the front half having gone to Barrow.

Needless to say the train was still packed so we bee-lined to the rear coach where the guard after a bit of vamping by a lady (in our estimation!) passenger decided to let us in also after enquiring if we carried a bottle of Scotch – we sorrowfully admitted the deficiency but confessed to having some wedding cake.

The baggage van was fairly well filled, with French sailors amongst others but we found a roomy stance near the 'cill' door (well grilled!).

And so to Carnforth where an elderly couple came up alongside our position. They were bound for the Brittania Inn, Elterwater for the weekend. They were both keen on mountaineering and had done their stuff in the past having been to Switzerland thirteen or so times. The man had met Whymper[2] twice in Switzerland – had climbed on Laddow, Castle Naze, Wales, LD and recommended the Isle of Arran. We gained a minor point by having climbed in Skye – an experience they both looked forward to. One interesting fact was divulged by the old boy – apparently he had heard by some means from Switzerland that the guides etc. expected to be able and ready to cater for mountaineers eighteen months after the end of the European War.

They left at Oxenholme. At Penrith I managed cups of tea and made a 'recky' down the train, spotting empty seats in the process. There wasn't time to get our rucksacks out and make a move but this was remedied at Carlisle and the rest of the journey was completed in comfort.

---

2. Edward Whymper (1840-1911) made the first ascent of the Matterhorn 14 July 1865.

During the baggage van episode we had a useful chat with the guard. Apparently the 4.03 connects with a train at Carstairs (normally leaves 10.25 but waits for the 4.03) which goes to Perth.

One changes at Stirling for a train which starts from there and goes to Oban via Crianlarich – reaching the former something after 5 a.m. and the latter something after 2 a.m. We decided to do this but after tipping up our half tickets and in order not to lower the prestige of Sassenachs in the eyes of the guard's assistant (real Scottish accent) who knew we had booked the George Hotel we decided to carry on with the original plan. Secondly we learned the 11.05 p.m. on Mondays and Fridays is regularly doubled – the first train leaving 11.05 for Liverpool and the second leaving 11.20 for Manchester There is one 'sleeper' for four first-class and twelve third-class passengers available only to 'high priority people or good liars'.

Left Carstairs 11.35 p.m. The weather was wet with low clouds up to Oxenholme (we thought of Oily & Alex 'hitching' and camping out and shuddered) but after crossing Shap the night was grand – stars, moon and all that! The run down to Glasgow in particular was grand in the moonlight. Arrived Glasgow 12.30 and beat it for the George Hotel and so to bed for 1 a.m. (Beds most comfortable.)

FRIDAY 30TH MARCH

Rose 5 a.m., after excellent 'night's' sleep, breakfasted off tea, bread & butter and paid bill 9/6 each plus 1/- tip – left 5.50 a.m. for Glasgow Queen St – plenty of room in saloon coach.

This train for some reason did not leave until 6.35 and thence followed an interesting pull up a steep incline with a fussy engine puffing and snorting along behind.

The usual gorgeous run up through the mountains ensued and we were thrilled to see our first mountain with snow on top. The Cobbler was similarly clad but the real stuff became evident when Crianlarich was reached.

At Crianlarich there ensued the usual hare down the platform to the refreshment room. Alan beat me to it but even his effort couldn't prevail against the handicap of starting from scratch due to being in the last coach – so four others beat us to the counter.

As we proceeded towards Tyndrum rain and sleet began to blow and snow fall at the higher altitudes. We left the LNER station at Tyndrum suitably battened down (having arrived about 9.15 a.m.) and crossed the valley to the LMS station from where we were told the bus to Glencoe started 10.30.

After receiving the permission of the stationmaster we proceeded to get the Primus stove going in the ladies' waiting room. The breakfast consisted of half a meat pie each and a boiled egg sandwich followed by toasted teacake with grapefruit marmalade & biscuits (also an Easter egg).

This was over by about 10.20 – more sleet fell and in fine periods the surrounding mountains looked fine in their cones of snow.

Time passed but still the bus didn't appear. We went to look for same only to be told by a chappie outside the local hotel that whilst the bus was bound to turn up they were having a little trouble five or so miles up the road – a little matter of a cracked cylinder head, he said! (Crikey!)

A bus appeared and we returned to the station. The bus was filled with a number standing and plenty of baggage in typical Highland fashion. It seemed full to us but some of the passengers assured us that more could be added if necessary.

A girl from Kinlochleven told me that she and parents had left that spot 5 a.m. the same morning with the idea of going to Edinburgh for the day. The bus stopped three times due to engine trouble and so they missed the train by 3 minutes – hence they were returning to Kinlochleven having had it!

We stopped at the truant bus just before Bridge of Orchy. Alan & I diagnosed fault in the low tension primary of the distribution system but on learning that our bus driver carried no tools of any description (my nail file was pressed into service to clean up the contact breaker points) it was decided to leave the poor thing and continue our journey.

All I saw thenceforth due to low windows and my standing position was grassy banks until we stopped again just beyond Kingshouse. Looking out I saw a terrific sight which I took to be Buachaille Etive – this was confirmed by two climber blokes who I learned had traveled up from Derby since the afternoon of yesterday and were going to stay at Clachaig Hotel.

One of them who was wearing glasses with thick black 'ear hooks' looked vaguely familiar and then I realized that he had given a lecture to the Rucksack Club some months earlier on local stuff. He confessed to this – also to an aversion to Poucher personally and told us that C. D. Milner was going to produce a book of mountain photographs entitled 'Mountain Photography' or somesuch – should be good.

Due to a number of questions I fear we left them with the impression that we were about to tackle the Crowberry Ridge under conditions which were, to say the least, fierce.

The bus stop was due to another bus (empty) putting in an appearance and for some reason we had to change into this bus so ours could I presume return to its ailing brother.

Altrafeadh was only ½ mile distant but even though this was to be our jumping off point we decided to ride.

Left the bus just after 1 p.m. – the single fare Tyndrum to Altrafeadh being 2/7 each.

Obtained permission (and key) to use 'Dan Mackay's' barn for lunch and proceeded to brew up. Lunch consisted of the usual brew, cheese & peanut butter sandwiches, jam sandwiches, biscuits.

Stob Dearg kept clearing and then becoming enveloped in snow clouds so we decided to attack it up the prominent gulley on the right which at the top looked well plastered with snow. On the way up we passed some slabby boiler plates which looked interesting but it was raining and we had already decided that leaving the road 2 p.m. meant that we could be back by 4.30 leaving 2½ hrs. for the 8-mile tramp to the Hostel.

Higher up the snow was falling and the climb up the last steep snow-covered section to the col was made more interesting by the occasional playful way the wind blew the surface snow into our faces. The time from the road to the col was 1 hour.

The wind was blowing hard snow fairly hard over the col and the view to the South looked forbidding – very black clouds with Glen Etive barely visible.

We continued up the ridge reaching the summit above the Crowberry ridge 3.25 – 1 hr. 25 mins. from the road – a vertical climb of 2,400 ft. We were lucky to have clear weather on the summit and whilst nothing could be seen to the South the views North to the Mamore Forest range and East over Rannoch Moor were a sight to gladden the eye. Snow-capped peaks with clouds above on the one hand and a 2,500 ft. drop to a large expanse of plain on the other.

We reluctantly decided that it was time to be on our way and so left 3.33. The drop down to the col was sudden but the passage down the steep top portion of the gulley was quicker – progress taking the form of sitting glissades.

Snow and sleet again fell during the descent so little time was lost and we hit the road 4.20 – 47 mins. from the top.

And so began the 8 miles hike – the packs were rather heavy and the sudden gusts of rain in our faces didn't help but the highest point of the pass 1,030 ft. was soon reached and the rest was all downhill (1 in 20 said the sign).

We followed the new road until just before the 'Study', where we changed to the old road and were rewarded with a fine view of the Three Sisters of Glencoe from the Study – they looked even better than depicted on excellent photographs.

The new road was rejoined immediately afterwards. This road incidentally seems to have been built absolutely ignoring the path of the old one and is a fine engineering job, the bridges especially. One theory is that the Macdonalds built the old road and a Campbell engineered the new ... The real reason is probably that the course of the old road was selected because it avoided the building of large bridges over the river – obviously a major issue with the ancients.

The Southern side of the pass looked really good but the Northern side was a little disappointing due to the presence of grassy slopes of an easier nature than one gathers from photographs.

We spotted Ossian's Cave and mentally made a note of a possible way up. The ridge above looked very inviting – steep snow-covered gullies leading on to what appeared to be a knife-edged ridge.

Just about here we received another lucky break in the form of a hitch from a Council lorry. This took us 2 or so miles to the road junction at the foot of Loch Triochatan. The wind had by this time almost dried our 'breeks' but as we expected the rains came on the last 2 miles to the Hostel. We arrived just before seven.

The Hostel was only partly filled – just comfortable in fact from the points of view of cooking and drying.

The Warden is a lady – we seemed to get on with her all right even though she took a poor view of most of the English hostellers (especially students) who stay at the Hostel and had an interesting discussion comparing the English and Scottish systems of running Hostels. She thought we had more discipline in our Hostels and naturally thought this a point in our favour.

Anyway the result was she gave us some oatmeal. Apparently we could get milk from the farm as a wretched calf, which some other wretch wouldn't take away, was consuming same at the rate of 2 galls. per day. Bread could be had but no potatoes so we were advised to pay a visit to the village store on the morrow.

Cooking on the stove (two available but the other unlit) was slow owing to the fire having been allowed to die down with four girls warming themselves before it – the soppy things! So we resorted to the Primus.

Our meal consisted of veg. soup, baked beans on toast, jam sandwiches & other odd things.

We had been advised that there would be about 100 in the Hostel Saturday night which made us thankful for the Primus. Alan retired about 10 p.m. and I followed after writing up the Chronicles about 11 p.m.

Note: Just beyond the road junction at the foot of Loch Triochatan we passed a sign erected by a motoring association commemorating the Massacre of Glencoe which was supposed to have occurred on that spot in 1692.

SATURDAY 31ST MARCH

Rose 8ish to the rhythm of the raindrops – good night's sleep. Breakfasted off porridge, bacon & fried spam, grapefruit marmalade & toast, ryvita & tea.

Left Hostel 11.30ish and sauntered down to Glencoe village – grand coniferous trees down the road – surprised to see the hawthorns brambles etc. more advance than in Sale. Bought candles, oatmeal & brown loaf in village store and noted announcement of dance in village hall for the same evening. Visited PO to see if view cards obtainable only to find it shut for lunch – looked in the church then walked down to Ballachulish–Kinlochleven crossroads.

Walked back by the new Glencoe road to the Hostel via wooden bridge across the Coe and through the woods.

The original intention to 'do' Aonach Dubh had dwindled to the mountain in front of the Hostel and finally as the rain continued to descend, and in view of the large invasion of the Hostel scheduled for that evening, this was jettisoned and we decided to stay in the Hostel, dry out and have the major meal when we got back.

This was about 1.30. The meal consisted of the usual soup, baked beans on toast, date sandwiches, tea & biscuits.

Following a chat with a Glasgow climber it was decided that we all move up to the Clachaig Hotel for tea – about 5.30.

Dinner being imminent we could only get tea & biscuits but since this was served in a very comfortable lounge with a large fire we didn't mind.

Two Scottish ladies and Sassenach friend provided very interesting conversation. Whilst everybody was at dinner we had a comfortable hour (with beer) around the fire.

With the return of the 'inmates' (including the two Derby climbers and a Glasgow laddie with a subtle sense of humour and obviously a true mountaineer) the conversation was again stimulating and general ranging from Youth Hostels through climbing advice – Pitlochry Hydro-Electric scheme to fairies and ghosts. There was the usual leg pulling of us Sassenachs with the superiority of Scots in England in little doubt!

I particularly liked the Glasgow climber's humorous description of an experience with an eagle on a climb – apparently it dropped down towards them like a plummet with a noise like a dropping boulder – they all flattened themselves to the rock face only to see a bird whiz past then calmly flatten out, fetch round, look at them as much to say 'that put the wind up you' and then sheer off.

We left 10 p.m. only to find everything pitch black outside – the mile return journey without a torch stretched the old sense of direction to the limit.

After a brew and a jam sandwich we found we had to transfer to the downstairs bedroom. This was straightened out and we retired 11 p.m.

SUNDAY 1ST APRIL

To make up for yesterday's laziness it was decided to make an early start and so we rose 7.15 once more after a good night's sleep and to the accompaniment of rain 'chatter'.

Let this go on record ... got the first fire going which was very satisfying to a mere Englander as the Scotty had one or two false starts with the other fire – the day was made!

Alan as usual manhandled the Primus and the cooking thereon whilst I looked after other incidentals.

Breakfast consisted of porridge (we seemed to be the only people in the Hostel having this Scottish delicacy!), baked beans on toast, tea.

We left 9.45 in momentary rainless weather but donned gas capes 5 minutes later. Leaving the road at the crossroads a course was set up the mountainside in driving rain to the waterfalls descending from the coire above and beneath the towering face of Aonach Dubh.

Above the waterfall we bore slightly right with a lovely snow chute as the major attraction. On the way up to this I found quite a whizzing stainless steel knife (this makes me all square as I lost a similar knife in the Lake District 3 years ago). The snow chute was lovely – it being necessary to kick steps up the last section.

Just before coming out on to the col between An t-Sron 2,715 ft. and Stob Coire nam Beith 3,621 ft. we had a peanut butter sandwich & chocolate. It had taken us 1¾ hrs. from the road.

The wind was quite cold and strong on the ridge and mixed with occasional hail as we made our way up to Stob Coire nam Beith, reaching same about 2¼ hrs. from the road. The rocks on the side of the prevailing wind (South) were glazed with ice and on the Northern side the ridge was deeply corniced with hard snow which continued downwards to form fine snow chutes.

We were in cloud all the time which made navigation with a ½-inch map and no compass quite tricky – the prevailing wind helped!

It was due to this that at this juncture we made our only 'blind' move. We thought we had been on Bidean nam Bian 3,766 ft. and were going North to Stob Coire nan Lochan 3,677 ft. but a glimpse of a valley to our left together with the direction of the snow cornices – the short distance covered and the small drop between the two indicated that were on Bidean nam Bian.

This was borne out by continuing East when we lost height rapidly and dropped down to a col at the head of valley which we recognised (from the map) as Allt Coire Gabhail.

We continued on and soon stood on the summit of Beinn Fhada (3,497 ft) where we collected specimens of a whitish marbley stone and a red stone.

Steps were retraced to the col and a super glissade (sitting at first followed by standing) made down into Allt Coire Gabhail.

This was a most attractive coire with the stream tumbling down a gorge and snow plastered gullies and rock faces at the head.

After about a mile the steep-sided coire leveled out to a flat Alpish sort of space at the mouth of the coire above the Pass of Glencoe.

There were trees (mostly silver birch) and large rocks left lying about the mouth of the coire and here we found a marvelous dry cave which judging by the quantity of empty tins had been used before. It was raining so we took shelter to 'brew up' and have lunch consisting of spam sandwiches, date sandwiches, tea & chocolate (and a cigarette for the 'lad') – this would be 3.15ish, the lunch taking about ½ hour.

We were told later by our Glasgow friend that this place was used by the MacDonalds for keeping their stolen cattle – there certainly was plenty of grass and the entrance could be held by a few men.

The drop down was a very interesting scramble – so much so that we decided to cross over to the left hand side – a manoeuvre which proved a little tricky in view of the swollen nature of the stream.

We dropped down quickly after a spot of 'recky' work to the River Coe – in fact Alan dropped down too quickly once and cut his hand on the ice axe!

At the junction of the Coire and stream coming down from Stob Coire nan Lochan we decided that the road above looked more attractive than the route along the base of the mountains. We didn't actually swim the stream but I, at least, realized the drawbacks of a 'runtish' stature – my rolled up shorts being just clear of the fast moving water. We hit the road about 4.45 and walked to the Hostel for 5.45.

Our meal consisted of veg. soup (2 tins), fried spam & cheese on toast, bread & jam, biscuits & tea.

We spent the evening in the Hostel (after I had made a sortie to gather some primrose roots) and very much alive it was with various groups singing very 'catchy' songs with in one case very good mouth organ accompaniment whilst I endeavoured to write up these Chronicles. It was a grand experience though and quite different to English Hostels.

The place was full to capacity (about) which rather emphasized the atmosphere – meal times in particular being well worth seeing with everybody manoeuvring for position (and pans) at the two stoves and others, in the know, using their Primus stoves. We retired 11.30 BDST.

MONDAY 2ND APRIL

Another early rise – 7.15 a.m. to weather which seemed a little better but windy and squally still. Breakfast off usual porridge, baked beans & bacon on toast, bread & butter, marmalade, tea etc.

Made up sandwiches since we intended traveling light and doing plenty before catching the afternoon bus, 4.30 p.m. – we originally intended to catch the 6 a.m. bus right down to Arrochar but this was jettisoned for obvious reasons on learning of this later connection via Tyndrum and Stirling to Glasgow.

Cleaned up both sinks (which were a greasy filthy mess!) as a chore and then collected our cards, duly stamped GLENCOE, packed our rucksacks ready for leaving in the afternoon and after making adieux to Warden and Glasgow friend we left the Hostel about 9.45 clad in shorts, gas cape etc. and carrying sandwiches in pockets.[3] We walked up the road almost to the Clachaig Hotel and then struck up the hillside making a beeline for the Southern ridge of the Western end of Aonach Eagach. Round the corner the wind (Westerly) wasn't so bad and except for a brief halt on my part continuous progress was made to the summit and we were soon in cloud. The sleet tap was turned on and it was not too warm.

In view of the conditions and also in view of the short time available it was decided to reach the highest point of the ridge and return instead of, as originally intended, traversing the ridge to Am Bodach and returning along the Pass of Glencoe.

The summit of Sgorr nam Fiannaidh was reached 12.20, 2 hrs. 20 mins. after leaving the road – an ascent of 3,000 ft. There was snow on the north face of this summit and we were granted a part view of the ridge (which looked very interesting further on) and a view of Loch Leven below – but only for a few minutes.

We ate our lunch of Spam & date sandwiches and left the summit about 12.40 p.m. after I had collected a 'specimen' of marble, or so it appeared!

We made good progress to the extreme Western end of the ridge and were soon below cloud level with the Hostel directly below us.

A beeline was made down a very steep slope which, due to the absence of heel and centre sole nails, slowed Alan quite a lot – by experiment he found it

---

3. See the List of Requirements for inventory of food and equipment taken.

quicker to come down backwards way! The views to the West were marvellous Loch Linnhe and the Garbh Bheinn group of mountains beyond standing out like a picture. From higher up the slope we also gathered a marvellous map-like impression of the valley connecting Glencoe to Loch Leven.

Arriving at the Hostel 1.30 we were able to make a good meal consisting of fried spam, dried egg (enough for four) and bread fried in the remaining fat, bread & butter & jam, tea.

Left a little 'latish' we thought 3.15 p.m. to walk to Ballachulish which we did in shorts because of the possibility of getting wet – actually we didn't. Passed Alan Small (JSMC Hon Sec) and camp follower on way and arrived Ballachulish 4 p.m.

Two buses left at 4.35 (one duplicate) – we on the second which left first! Of course our inevitable little gang of Glasgow toughs was in the back of the bus and entertained us to a spot of singing. We were able to sit and as far as rain and misty windows permitted managed glimpses of the mountains we had been on. Buchaille Etive looked impressive and Rannoch Moor forbidding.

Arrived Tyndrum 6ish. After a false alarm in the shape of an express (nifty bit of key exchanging here) – the Glasgow stopper arrived (late of course) and we continued on a rattling but from a scenery point of view terrific journey via Stirling to the City. The run down towards the plains around Stirling made up for the lack of vistas over the weekend with the setting sun shining on flooded rivers and ploughed fields etc.

During the latter part of this journey a young bloke in spectacles and overcoat with a pair of climbing boots in one hand *engaged* us in conversation (we were sitting first class by this time having stood in the corridor some while). Turned out to be Glasgow Univ. student (Arts) and the laddie who came off Aonach Eagach with teeth chattering and all – conversation indicated lack of experience – apparently a member of the JSMC. Incidentally we learned that this club had been holding a 'meet' at Glencoe that weekend – Scottish individuality making itself felt with this bloke at Ballachulish –

five blokes at Clachaig 4 or 5 miles away and three more at Kingshouse a further 10 miles on – strangely enough I don't believe they ever met!

Arrived Buchanan St. 9.30ish – quite a decent queue waiting at ten to ten for the 11.10 train so Alan bagged a place whilst I foraged without much success (glass of mineral and ten cigs)

Train left pretty well on time – four of us in a compartment – rear of train full as usual. Two other middle-aged blokes in the compartment seemed 'sporty' and on our mention of a Primus said 'looks like we can expect some tea later on.' That was all we wanted and, probably to their surprise, we started making preparations for brewing up in the compartment.

Alan spilling some water on the floor out of the mess tin, we expected some trouble with the thing on the Primus due to rocking of the train. Fortunately the train slowed down a bit and the water was heating up nicely when one of our compartment 'mates' observed 'you'd better hurry up, we start going downhill shortly'.

And we did! – after the overflow had extinguished the Primus and added to the water content of the floor we put the remaining water in my enamel mug and soon managed a full mug of tea without any more trouble. Our 'mates' refused our offer of a drink either out of politeness or because they had seen it made – very likely the latter!

After mopping up operations Alan went to sleep. At the next stop Carlisle two chaps got in and then I remembered no more until Alan woke me up in Exchange station at 7.45.

And so ended a very successful and interesting weekend during which a useful amount of mountaineering was done (five Munros) much knowledge gained and everything went according to plan.

Alan and Harry on Scafell Pike, November 1942.

LIST OF REQUIREMENTS
FOR GLENCOE EXPEDITION

HARRY

WEAR – green trilby and chin strap, brown jacket, green roll neck, brown 'trous', brown shoes (latest), brown socks, blue striped shirt, wool undervest and pants, belay, Karabiner.

CARRY – wallet, postcards and stamps, pen, money, penknife, comb, handkerchief, tobacco, pipe, matches, lighter, keys, watch (egg boiler) on leather strap, ice axe, note book.

RUCKSACK – **Back pocket:** climbing boots, grey oversocks. **Offside pocket:** Primus stove filled with paraffin, bottle of paraffin, bottle of meths. **Nearside pocket:** oil skin, enamel mug. **Inside:** woollen gloves, pyjamas, shorts, spare shirt, black stockings, Harris stockings, towel, pullover, sheet sleeping bag. Camera and exposure table, map of Br. Isles, Barths maps of Perth and Glencoe, SMC guide.

WATERPROOF BAG – razor, brush, shaving soap, tooth brush, tooth paste (Al tin), soap, burn oil, elastic bandage, ordinary bandage, Elastoplast, cotton wool, Boracic lint. **Food etc:** knife, folk, dessert spoon, teaspoon, soup dish. Loaf, sandwiches, marg, lard, ½ lb. peanut butter, sugar, tin soya cream, two tins vegetable soup, two tins beans, one tin spam, ½ lb. cheese, dates, Ryvita, bacon, chocolate, salt.

ALAN

He carried the rope, his personal effects and in addition his share of the food consisted of:

Loaf, sandwiches, tin dried milk, tin soup, Oxo cubes, pkt. dried eggs, 6 ozs. tea, sugar, butter, lard, tin pork luncheon meat, tin sardines, 1 lb. tin marmalade, pot of jam, bacon.

PILLAR ROCK, WHITSUN 1943.

WASDALE

WHITSUNTIDE 1945

THURSDAY 24TH MAY

At 4 p.m. I turned away from the Works with a silent tear, mounted the 'cellar' model and pedalled with decorum to Exchange Station. There was plenty of room on the train at this hour (4.30) so after depositing the model in the for'ard baggage compartment I found a 'third' in the coach next the engine. A KMC member, George Stonely, was already in possession.

Had a 'cuppa' and returned collecting Norman[1] & Bob Stevens on the way. Things were filling up by this time – another KMC member turned up, 'Ferdi', and was duly advised of the lashings of room in the corridors!

Geoff Hallawell was also seen with lady friend, and pals ditto. They as a consequence (of well what do you think?) were taking a gentleman's holiday and staying at the Langdales Hotel.

The departure of the train at 5.10 was hardly noticed as by this time a discussion between Bob Sevens & self on the prospects of Labour and Conservatives in the coming election was well under way.

The compartment was next treated (!) to details of rock climbs and a tentative start was made in the gentle art of pulling of Bob's extensible leg. After some time a bloke in the corner joined in and proved himself a dormant member of the Rucksack Club (fortunately we had refrained from any of our usual references to the inactivities of this group of 'past glories').

---

1. Norman L. Horsfield, founder member of the Karabiner Mountaineering Club.

He shot a few lines – 'the 500 ft, ¼-inch wire hawser used for potholing which came up like knitting and filled the cabin'. We got one useful piece of gem from him – a certain ointment used by the Army for the successful warding off of affectionate mosqis and other insects (paraffin can be used, but the smell is less tolerable than the insect bites!)[2]

The weather was just perfect as we sped across the level stretch before Lancaster – plenty of sun clear sky etc. At Carnforth the lads got the tea situation organised (we had eaten after Preston) and brought six cups.

Between Kendal and Windermere Ferdi joined us and seemed a bit concerned as to how he and Audrey were to get to Wall End Farm, Ambleside. The problem was solved when Norman returned to say that Geoff and lady etc. were taxi-ing to the Langdales – Ferdi fixed up to share their taxi.

Immediately afterwards THE GREAT THOUGHT occurred – why shouldn't said taxi carry Norman's and my rucksack – t'was soon arranged just in time to beat Bob to it. He seemed to think we might help he and George up the steep bits on the cycle run to the Robertson Lamb Hut but we gently pointed out that we were walking to Wasdale that night and he wasn't. 'Oh, of course, I forgot'.

We arrived Windermere 8.45 and taxis were sought. Ferdi & Audrey had to share a taxi with two others – a detail which didn't worry *us*, they had Norman's rucksack. ('Oh Ferdi here's your other rucker.') Geoff carried my rucker on his knee. One thing however did please us – the KMC (and our ruckers) were traveling in state – two Rolls Royces!

The scenery looked superb in the evening sun as we speeded towards Langdale passing Bob & George on the way. ('You poor boys – these packs must be heavy.')

2. Di Methyl Phthialate – liquid-odourless – lasts approx 3 hrs., sprinkled on. Useful as protection against mosquitoes, mites, gnats – used by Army in Burma. Information supplied by 'Beard' at Brackenclose.

A large arrow with 'KMC' on the roadway at the Elterwater crossroads indicated the portion of wall behind which Norman's rucksack lay.

I called in at the Langdales and found Geoff and was introduced to the 'ladies' as the bloke who was going to have a 'do' at the hardest climb in Great Britain or something – no wonder one of them said 'Harry I wish I had a red complexion like yours.'(Pity Geoff is tied down – as an expert amateur photographer he seemed very keen to come over and 'shoot' our antics on Scafell.)

After passing Ferdi & Audrey we called in at RLH, had a few words with Bob & George and continued to Wall End. We parked our bikes in the top barn to find 'Stony' and other members of the KMC already in residence, after which we sauntered down to the farm to don our boots and have coffee & sandwiches.

Young 'Zech' (the farmer's son and the cause of the uproarious twenty-first do last Christmas) turned up on a 1939 500 cc Triumph which was duly admired.

During conversation with Mrs Myers & old 'Zech' we learned of the VE Day happenings at the Old Dungeon Ghyll Hotel. As Bulman had promised all drinks (of every type) were free on the house all day – oddly enough the place was crowded all day!

The light was still good and the nearly full moon visible as we left for Wasdale 16 mins. to 10 p.m.

All the surrounding peaks looked good – being clear cut against the sky as we trudged up to Rossett Ghyll. As to Rossett Ghyll – nuff said! – it was a sweat until we began to get our second wind and generally limber up.

The reflected light on Angle Tarn was a grand site – quite amber in colour.

Esk Hause was reached after about 2 hrs. We rested a short while then beat it for Sty Head and so down under Gable (This time I wasn't scared out of my skin halfway down – a nasty thing to happen!)

Passing Burnthwaite 1 a.m.(ish) we audibly regretted the starting of the last Severe climb just as it was getting dark – we hope any of the inhabitants who happened to be awake were impressed!

Just afterwards a bloke on a cycle passed us going Gosforth way ('Dratted cyclist, worse than Manchester.'). The place seemed lousy with cycle pushers – we were next passed by a girl going towards Wasdale Head who was followed at a short distance by the first bloke we had seen – 'the goings on in Wasdale!'

The last mile to Brackenclose was rather humdrum – one might almost say we were beginning to tire! Arrived at the hut 1.25 a.m.

After a 'cuppa' and a bite we retired 2.30 a.m. 'The hours some people keep!'

FRIDAY 25TH MAY

Needless to say we slept rather soundly until being awakened by some louts at 6 a.m. – no Christian people would get up at this hour!

We arose about 8.45 a.m. and found that approx. eight other 'blokes' and one 'blokess' were in residence.

Whilst Norman organised breakfast cooking I went down to the Martin's farm – collected a pint of milk *and* a doz. eggs (3d each)

After a good breakfast consisting of porridge, sausage & egg, toast, jam and the inevitable tea we left 11.05 a.m. for Pillar.

In passing I might mention one of the inmates – a rather superior type with whom we had a subtle wording dual – understatement v superior knowledge. 'Did you get lost last night?' 'No we only left Manchester 5 p.m. yesterday afternoon and walked over from Langdale!' The other blokes were rather unassuming and seemed slightly under the thumb of the 'big cheese'.

We called in at Mrs Naylor's to pay our respects, leave a PO for collection and prepare the ground for the acquisition of bread & butter. Incidentally we learned that our girl cyclist of the early morning was Mrs. Naylor's daughter Margory returning from a dance at Gosforth – some teasing ensued.

It was rather close with plenty of cloud about as we wended are way up Black Sail Pass. Just before gaining the Pillar ridge the rains came – nice and steady, in the Lakeland refined manner.

Our ambitions of 'doing' *Walkers Gully* began to fade.

Following the high level route we reached the foot of Pillar Rock 1.30ish – 2½ hrs. out, not bad going.

After a bite we roped up and I ran about 100 ft. out up the first two pitches until the disappearance of the good holds near the finish of pitch 2.

Decided to bring Norman up and he reached the top of pitch 2 by attaining the terrace by the easier way. I followed by the same route and continued to the 'exposed trough with very poor holds'. It was very cold to the hands due to wet rock, cold breeze and slight water precipitation.

I didn't like the exposed trough a bit under these conditions, and after discussion with Norman we decided, in view of the fact that the worst pitch was the last one, to beat a retreat and live to fight another day.

We looked at Shamrock Gully but after finding out that at least 500 ft. of climbing was involved we thought that in view of the last strenuous 14 hrs., to climb to the top of Pillar and descend to Mosedale via the scree from Windy Gap.

This was done. There was plenty of cloud about but it was not raining and still much warmer in Mosedale than on the other side of Pillar.

We reached Mrs Naylor's about 4.30 and partook of a pot of tea and cleaned up our sandwiches. An interesting discussion at the table ensued on the merits of Americans with a bloke who started life in Ireland went to America and then returned to this country. Quite an intelligent sort of chappie (he agreed with us).

The bloke put in an appearance who according to Mrs Naylor had paid her that morning a week in advance because he was going to have a do for the first time at this climbing racket with two other chaps – apparently his fears were ungrounded!

Norman told me afterwards of one of this laddies' strange theories in regard to climbing – apparently it should be no more difficult making a tricky move 10 ft. up than 1,000 ft. up!

The weather by this time was glorious and we were able to put our wet stuff out on the hut steps to dry.

Dinner consisted of pea soup, egg & cheese, toast with the usual jam bread & butter and spot of cake to follow.

Norman went to see if Ferdi & Audrey had arrived at the barn whilst I started the Chronicles. He returned to report no sign – can this be weakening of the Karabiner?

After a 'cuppa' we retired about 11 p.m.

SATURDAY 26TH MAY

No disturbers of the peace this morning but even we thought 8.45 wasn't too late to get up.

I shook Norman (and myself) by having a cold shower.

Breakfast consisted of porridge (good), bacon & egg, sausage, toast & jam, tea.

We left about 11 a.m. in warm sunshine, going via Wasdale Hotel in order that I could post cards to mother & Margot (really hectic oil painting 'dos').

We passed the 'big cheese' at Burnthwaite who had come up solo on a cycle and was apparently going on Boat Howe – we didn't think it wise to enquire if he was going there alone!

The climb up Gavel Neese was uneventful but as always still a sweat – the sun helped in this direction even though there were plenty of white and off white clouds around.

The reader may be relieved to learn that I had forgotten to take my watch – hence no time statistics.

A bite was had and then we roped up at the foot of the *Arrowhead Direct*. Norman led to the top of pitch 1 and I followed thro' to lead pitch 2 – at least that was the idea but the move round the corner seemed to lack a handhold and I lacked courage – after two 'dos' followed by pauses to warm up the old hands it started to rain. The thought of wet handholds must have spurred me on because I was round the corner and up in two, or possibly three, blinks of an eyelid.

Norman came up to my stance at the foot of the slab pitch leading to the base of the Arrowhead. By this time there was hail mixed up with the rain – which was in earnest. I then led up the slab which was getting wetter and wetter – stuck halfway up by the lack of faith in a wet key handhold. After experimenting for some time with again repeated step downs to warm hands (and regain leg control) I found a useful foothold and was soon up to the base of the Arrowhead.

Taking a poor view of the frontal ascent of the Arrowhead in its present rather supersaturated condition I decided to traverse round the side and gained the top of the back. Belayed on to the top (pure showmanship!) and brought Norman up for him to lead through. The rest of the climb was uneventful.

A return to the base was made and we had a few sandwiches at the foot of Abbey Buttress.

The rain was real Lake District stuff still as we made our way to the Needle.

Not wasting any time since by this time we were rather wet and getting wetter I went up the Arête to the Shoulder – belayed and Norman followed.

Attaining the Mantelshelf was easy and the traverse left to the corner was easy but when it came to making the high step up with holds which, on a fine day, leave much to be desired, well, I thought better of it – a slip of the left boot which was supporting most of my weight didn't improve my outlook either.

I returned to the Shoulder and much to Norman's amusement went all Wild West and endeavoured to throw the rope over the block – without avail.

Another attempt was made but we were getting colder and it was still raining so we decided to return to the bottom. Norman went down Lingmell Crack and reached the base after a bit of a hiatus near the bottom (the cold was making itself felt).

We soon warmed up with the scree run down to the Sty Head path.

A lady walker passed and asked us if we had been rained off – since the rain by this time had ceased it looked more like we had been 'fired off'!

We made a beeline for Mrs Naylor's to stand in front of her glorious gigantic anthracite stoked cooker (all singing and dancing!). Tea was served up and more teasing of Marjory took place. After scrounging another 2 lb. loaf (actually Mrs Naylor said that if we had written she could have made arrangements to provision us) we returned to Brackenclose with signs of rain over Wast Water (about 6.30 p.m.).

The 'big cheese' and his three accomplices were using the common room fire for drying, the excuse being the necessity of packing clothing. Anyway we decided in view of the number of wet things to light the drying room fire.

This was done and the more serious business of cooking embarked upon.

The 'beard' gave us some potatoes which were incorporated in the kidney soup. The next course was a tremendous one of baked beans, egg & fried spam. 'Beard' gave us some cold rice & red currant puree (for children, vitamin C and all that) which proved very good.

Norman wandered down to the farm for milk whilst I wrote up the Chronicles.

Whilst this was in progress a chap and wife put in an appearance – Wayfarers from Yorkshire, Middlesborough way.

A grand fug by this time was generated in the drying room.

Following a 'cuppa' we turned in something after 11 p.m.

Sunday 27th May

Getting up time was usual 8.30 – 'usual' cold shower.

Took all surplus bread (a tin full) down to the farm and collected 1 pint of milk & a doz. eggs – (just like that) whilst Norman got cracking on breakfast. This consisted of porridge – egg, breakfast meat & cheese – toast & jam with some Ryvita biscuits (salvaged) thrown in.

Cleared up the fireplace, re-laid the fire and swept out common room, entrance hall, drying room and kitchen. Made sandwiches, filled in all the appropriate books and forms, collected our gear and left 11.10ish.

Plenty of cloud about and an Eastish wind as we plodded up Brown Tongue to Scafell. Reached *Rake's Progress* in about 1 hr. 40 and partook of lunch at the foot of *Botterill's Slab* – a fearsome looking climb!

Lead up first three pitches of Moss Ghyll in one (100 ft.) and with Norman belayed went up first pitch (60 ft.) of *Moss Ghyll Grooves* to ledge on level of the Oval where a suitable belay 'was arranged'.

Norman came up without any trouble and passed along to the Oval underneath the Flake on the *Central Buttress* climb.

After attending to a small matter I followed to join Norman and pay respectful attention to *the* pitch on *CB*.

The thinnest parts of the climb looked wet and we felt, if we didn't look, cold, so we decided not to have a 'do' (we were still in boots, our rubbers having reposed peacefully in our rucksacks all the last three days).

I toyed with the idea of continuing up the *Grooves*, liking the look of same, but the weather looked uncertain and so we returned down to *Moss Ghyll* – not without a little trepidation on my part, I never did like climbing down this pitch in boots!

Reached the foot of *Moss Ghyll* just in time – hailstones descended to be followed by the more steady rain.

We passed along *Rake's Progress* to Mickledore and so up to Scafell Pike for 3.50 p.m.

Two people were in possession who after suitable advice from the 'experts' descended to the Corridor Route to return to Borrowdale.

The rain had ceased by this time and the views from Scafell to the West, North and East were good as seen under a ceiling of cloud some one or two thousand feet higher than the mountains.

We quitted Scafell 4.02 p.m. (BDST) and made good progress to Esk Hause passing a few people on the way.

Our packs weighed somewhat and we had a 5 minutes' respite at Esk Hause before carrying on to the top of Rossett Ghyll where another 5 minutes' pause was enjoyed.

We tore down Rossett Ghyll reaching the divergence of the Rossett and

Stake Pass paths in 20 mins.

The tramp along the valley floor on springy turf was a sheer joy after the jarring of the higher altitude part of our trek.

After passing thro' Stool End Farm the rains came and it may have been due to this or it may have been sheer bravado, but we ran most of the last two or three hundred yards reaching Wall End 2 hr. 8 mins. from Scafell Pikes.[3]

Coffee was absorbed after which we went to dig out the cycles. I was annoyed to find my front wheel buckled but fortunately the model was still rideable – apparently one of Karabiner boys had had a spill.

We reached the Fell & Rock hut (Row Head) just after 7 p.m. to find the place locked up.

An entrance was gained via the front veranda and bedroom window employing a sort of mantelshelf technique.

By the time member Kenyon put in an appearance we were established.

The hut is quite different to Brackenclose being an old farm house. The adaption has been very well done and the place is very attractive. The beds are more of the Youth Hostel type, is what we can only expect in war time.

I went up to Mickleden Farm for two pints of milk whilst Norman as usual busied himself with cooking in his efficient manner. Jack Cook was apparently not in residence.

After an excellent meal consisting of pea soup, egg, spam & cheese, malt loaf & dates, bread & butter – tea we repaired to the New Dungeon Ghyll to greet Albert Black, the 'prop' in the bar.

He told us that Jack Cook had just returned from Skye and was at Wall

---

3. Approximately 10,500 ft. climbed and 35 miles walked in three days.

End so, after coaxing out of him the key of the Wayfarers' Club hut in order that the alarm clock could be borrowed, we repaired thither.

I had a good chat with Jack during which I learned that he had had good weather and had met Poucher who was gathering photographs for a new book on Skye. Jack and his friends had apparently posed for Poucher to give scale to some of the shots.

After exchanging greetings with Audrey, 'Ferdi' & 'Stony' in the lower barn we returned to Row Head where after collecting the alarm clock, we turned in about 11 p.m.

MONDAY 28TH MAY

The fun and games started at 4.20 a.m. (again BDST) with the raucous clamour of the Wayfarers' alarm clock. The thing soon stopped but, as I feared, after a short silence it went again and there was no means of rendering it inoperative. I wrapped the clock up in a towel dashed down stairs and deposited it in the kitchen which seemed the spot furthest from the other 'sleepers'. On returning to the dormitory I could still hear its melodious tones. This struck me as funny and I laughed, the sound of which must have been the last straw for Kenyon who was sharing our dorm and a short irate cross talk ensued. 'Why don't you stop it ringing?', 'I can't it is a repeater', 'It is your business to do something' – silence – not the sort of bloke for an early Alpine start!

I returned the now silent clock to the Wayfarers' hut and then cycled up to the New Dungeon Ghyll hotel to return the key whilst Norman prepared breakfast.

Carrying out the miscellaneous chores allotted to me I endeavored to fill the tea pot only to find the kettle empty (being cast iron its weight is misleading). Not being the time of the morning for bright thoughts I promptly ran cold water into the kettle. Now I don't blame the kettle for what was after all a perfectly natural phenomenon, but the steam generated *did* scald three fingers of my right hand! Added to which I daren't drop the thing for fear of breaking the wash sink below. Great self-control was shown I thought – only two swear words being uttered, although I must admit they were expressive!

Breakfast – porridge, egg, cheese & spam, bread jam, tea.

We left about 5.25 and cycled down the valley, Norman having a little difficulty with his three-speed which would only work in top and slipped occasionally at that – a playful whimsy which takes on a different aspect at that time in the morning.

We were making good time at Ambleside having ½ hr. in hand and more than half the journey completed. The uphill work to Windermere however necessitated much walking (i.e cycling uphill in top gear isn't nice!).

With 10 minutes to go we were still quite a distance from the station so, since it was important I catch the 6.30 train, I pushed on ahead to continue an uphill grind against time. Arrived on platform 6.29½ – arranged to hold up the train 3 mins. but Norman didn't appear and the guard wouldn't wait any longer so off we went. Actually Norman reached the platform 6.35 and later caught the 8 a.m. arriving in Manchester about 10.30.

The first 5 or 10 mins. in the train were rather painful – the cooling wind during the cycle ride had kept the temperature of my fingers down. Rather large water blisters were in evidence but during the first lull I put some acriflavine on my fingers which eased things tremendously. Actually I experienced no more trouble and had them treated with burn ointment, violet, and bandaged up at the Works.

Changed at Carnforth to a train from Barrow which fortunately stopped at Eccles so that I was able to reach the office 9.50 a.m.

RATAGAN YOUTH HOSTEL, LOCH DUICH.

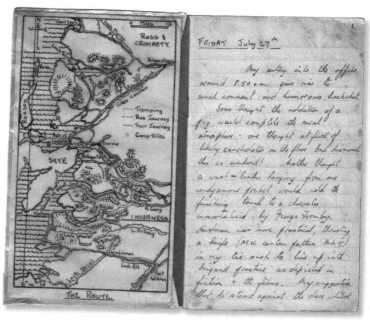

Top: This fine-looking Scot is the present warden at Ratagan YH.
Bottom: Sketch map of the expedition and the first page of the Chronicle.

Loch Shiel –
Torridon Expedition

August 1945

Friday 27th July

My entry into the office around 8.50 a.m. gave rise to much comment and humorous backchat. Some thought the addition of a pig would complete the rural atmosphere – one thought at first of likely candidates on the floor but dismissed this as unkind! Another thought a wash-leather hanging from one windjammer pocket would add the finishing touch to a character immortalised by George Formby.

Hardman was more practical, thrusting a knife (MV canteen pattern Mk2) in my tie sash to line up with brigade practice as depicted in fiction and the films. My suggestion that he stand against the door whilst I endeavoured to stick the knife from long range in the woodwork as near one 'ear'ole' as possible was received with little enthusiasm.

The piece of tree deputising as a tent pole however led the popularity poll.

During the morning made a trip into D Aisle for the purpose of having rucksack (complete) weighed. The result was very satisfying – being spot on the figure decided beforehand as a 'reasonable' amount for carrying – 30 lbs.

Sent telegram to the postmaster at Achnashellach at lunch time asking him to keep the parcel addressed to the Youth Hostel (closed) for our arrival on Wednesday next.

Things were rather hectic after lunch, adding the final touches to a USSR

Hydro Station tender which I wanted to get away to the Ministry of Supply before leaving. This and one or two other things (including a 'cuppa' shared with the 'lads') were achieved but it put the time on to 3.10 p.m. before I could get away. Much to my (and everyone else's) amusement I found my 'tree' adorned with a notice pointing out that this pole was not for opening and shutting the office windows!

The bus queue at the North Gate of the Works looked a little too long for my liking. The bus finally arrived 3.20 and fortunately it was an 84 and more fortunately, as events transpired the guard was a 'lady' – a real 'un! This became evident after I had been on the top of the bus, found it full and returned to the platform to find the dear girl ordering the excess off the bus. Two blokes who followed me down meekly got off but I was getting a bit desperate so I pitched a story about the train for Scotland backed up by a very appealing look. First of all she let me stay on then, two women, who were well established the b-----s, muttered about their having a train to catch also, the guard ordered me off. Again I switched on the appeal and at last she found an excuse – hadn't I been upstairs and therefore must have been in front of the others who had gone inside – yes of course – and 'on' I stayed.

We were quite 'pally' by the time Manchester was reached – apparently she had saved my rucksack from falling off the bus twice and played 'old Harry' with a bloke in connection with same.

Whilst we were talking, waiting for passengers to alight another noise arose – apparently the two b-----s once more had a train to catch and their suitcases were underneath my rucksack!

Bob had saved me a seat at the rear of the train and we left on time 4.03 p.m. The train was full but not overcrowded i.e. there was still room to stand in the corridor and the luggage van was quite unused (yet).

At Preston the train pulled in with our coach opposite the refreshment room for which I bee-lined with me billy can in me 'and. A few wisecracks but the result was quite satisfactory – half full with good looking tea and plenty of sugar. Our giving a middle-aged lady opposite (school teacher?)

first swig (I'll bet she hadn't drunk out of a large enamel mug for some time) later reaped dividends. I was debating aloud with Bob the prospects of getting cigarettes (we were still in Preston) when she offered me ten Capstan – new and untouched – the offer was gratefully taken up. Bob I think was also offered one but apparently he still does not smoke.

We stopped at Carnforth, Oxenholme (the Lakeland hills looked fine: Coniston Old Man, Pikes, Gable etc. being easily seen), Penrith, Carlisle (more tea!), Lockerbie, Beattock, Carstairs and finally arrived Glasgow ½ hr. late at 11.25 p.m. Checked into the George (same night porter) and were in bed 11.45 having recorded our need for a call at 4.45 a.m. the following morning.

Note: Weather fine on the way up – one slight effort at rain but clouds broken up and at medium height.

SATURDAY 28TH JULY

Called to time and out of bed for 4.50 to find the weather still behaving – no rain but cloudy. With Bob's help put a fresh dressing on my arm using the material supplied by the Ambulance Room nurse in the Works.

Usual snack of tea (strong), bread & butter which extended its scope a little to take in more bread, tea & some marmalade after Bob had paid the bill and given the bloke a tip which was intended to be 2/-, but turned out to be 3/ – by the simple expedient of the porter forgetting to give us the 1/ – change due from the £1 handed over in payment for the bill.

We left 5.30 a.m. – bought papers, collected our single tickets and found good seats in the last coach on the train. This was late in starting – instead of 6.10 it was 6.48 before we left. The delay however gave me a chance of starting and bringing up to date this 'write up'.

The morning by this time was gorgeous – almost cloudless sky and, of course, plenty of sunshine.

As we travelled along between Dunbarton and Helensburgh we could see a number of vessels anchored off Gourock – these included two aircraft carriers – other warships and the *Queen Mary* with plenty of smoke belching from her three funnels (we knew she was the *Queen Mary* – the Scottish *Daily Express* told us so, kindly helping by giving a photograph; apparently she was ready to take 15,000 American soldiers back home.)

The next engineering matter of interest was the naval base built for the US navy on the shores of Gare Loch – a marvellous layout of sidings etc.

After the Cobbler came another engineering 'marvel' – just a number of cabins and a few excavations indicating that civil engineers were starting work on the hydro-electric power scheme which will utilize the water from Loch Slay to generate some 130,000 kW of electricity (later I learned from George Peat that this was a max demand and the station would operate on only 9% load factor – technical note!).

Crianlarich was reached and the usual beeline made for the refreshment room where tea awaited our billycans and sandwiches & scones were also available.

We availed ourselves of this service and returning along the platform encountered a bloke with friend whom Bob had met in Skye last year. These were George Peat & Jimmy Stuart, both SMC men and Hon Pres and Hon Vice Pres respectively of the Edinburgh section of the Junior SMC The other good lad Archy Nendy who was with George in Skye was unfortunately not present. They came along to our coach and an interesting talk ensued on principally climbing and hydroelectric matters. George told us a few interesting things about the application of the latter in Scotland gained during his work as a Civil Engineer.

And so Fort William was reached to be followed soon after by Glenfinnan at the head of Loch Shiel where Bonnie Prince Charlie set up his standard 200 years ago this year. Here we bad goodbye to George & Jimmy who were going to Glenbrittle and left the station 12.30 p.m.

We turned left down the road to Fort William, which we left opposite the sawmill, to follow a road which petered out after passing under the railway viaduct but gave way to a track leading up Glen Finnan. Here a small boy joined us and stayed just long enough to explain that the mysterious dug out in the hill side across the way was an air raid shelter!

After about ½ hr. going over flat but in places marshy land we stopped at an attractive spot in the river for lunch. The attraction about the river was its rocky bed which was water worn in quite fantastic shapes and provided excellent pools for bathing – the hint was taken!

We were to see a number of incidences of this phenomenon before the day was out (rock shapes I mean, not bathing beauties!).

A brew was made and various things including tomatoes, veal & ham pie, sausages, bread & butter etc. were absorbed into the human machines.

We continued on the steady trek (starting about 2.15) up the Glen to the Bealach between Sgur Thuilm and Streap. The Bealach (pass to you) at 1,536 ft. was reached about 4 p.m. where a short halt was made (there had been a pause on the way up).

We dropped down to fairly level ground in Glen a'Chaorainn in short time where we encountered a bearded Highlander complete with kilt and hung about with all sorts of impedimenta – such as tin for milk on side, tin with dry clothing in front, service gas mask case on other side (presumably without gas mask) and sleeping bag round waist under lumber jacket – oh I nearly forgot – he also had a rucksack on his back!

Apparently he had started from Ullapool 7 or 8 days ago and was making for Glenfinnan where he hoped to get a hitch. He was wearing shoes owing to blisters on feet rendering the wearing of his climbing boots, early on in the trip, impossible. He was pretty weary – and no wonder! After giving us some interesting information about the 'accommodation' he had found every night of his journey we said cheerio and continued on *our* journey at good speed down the rather monotonous (in my opinion) 2 or 3 miles to Strathan.

At Strathan they had just finished shearing some sheep and as we turned up Glen Dessarry the sheep were turned loose to stream in file across the bridge provided for them.

We were overtaken at Glendessary House by a young chap who had been helping with the shearing. He told us there were 8,000 sheep on the farm with hillsides capable of supporting 20,000. Bidding him goodnight we continued another mile and a half to Upper Glendessary (a small croft) where we had words with the good lady – a typical Highlander. Our enquiry re. milk was readily met – we had a glass each and nearly filled the billycan but the lady wouldn't accept payment so Bob hit on the bright idea of offering a bar of chocolate for 'the family' – the offer was accepted.

We continued ½ mile and selected a good spot at a bend in the river for the camp site – the time was something after 7 p.m.

Soup with meat and things – tea etc. were had – I dressed my arm and after doing a spot of Chronicles we turned in 10 p.m. (Earliest ever for me on a mountaineering holiday!)

SUNDAY 29TH JULY

Although we each wakened once or twice during the night we had no difficulty in getting to sleep again. In view of the fact that it was 9.15 a.m. before we finally decided to get up perhaps justifies our claim to a good night's sleep.

Porridge for breakfast with the excellent milk we had was marvellous – this was followed by bacon & egg (real!) & tomato with bread, butter & marmalade to finish off (and of course tea). We refrained from having a 'dip' although nearby there was an excellent channel worn out of the rock by the river.

It would be 11ish when we broke camp and started off up the glen. There was a track but this had a habit of disappearing. The summit of the Pass at 1,000 ft. was reached with, except for the usual water logged stretches, surprisingly little trouble.

Except for a little mix up around Lochan a'Mhaim where we became involved in many boulders, the journey down Mam Na Cloich Airde was reasonable going. This Pass was more impressive than the one we passed thro' yesterday due to many outcrops of rock and some towering rock faces.

The finish was even better for soon we could see Loch Nevis with its brown seaweed covered shores.

Reaching the head of the Loch we met our first inhabited house where we had words with an old lady who had quite a sense of humour. She recalled the mistaken bombing of Loch Nevis with zest and in response to our query as to the possibility of getting milk at the shepherd's house round the corner (info. from the bearded Highlander) on the Sabbath she confided in us that they were RC's (and she turned for him!).

Trudging round the headland we finally reached Carnoch and the shepherd's hut where we decided to lunch (1.30 to 2 p.m.).

We asked for milk of the shepherd's wife and of course plenty was forthcoming, we each being given two glasses. She also kindly gave us a billycan full for carrying onto the next camp site. It was drizzling a little by this time and we were invited into the 'parlour' to have our lunch. Half way thro' the meal our hostess produced a good-sized pat of home-made butter which we attacked with relish.

When we left, the children who were very shy on our arrival gave us repeated 'goodbyes' – possibly they had eaten our gift of chocolate by this time!

There was a steady drizzle as we tramped up the rather swampy valley of the River Carnoch. As we approached the last bend before the lochans the valley became very interesting with steep tree-clad sides. The scene at the point where we struck up the hillside might have been from Dovedale except the rock wasn't limestone.

It was hereabouts that we saw our first deer.

The track leading up to the pass opposite Ben Aden (a peaky mtn.) was an amazing affair being made up all the way and zigzagging like fury all the way up to the pass ('a regular old woman's do'). Shooting down the other side of the pass we were soon rewarded with a view of Loch Hourn.

We had already decided that to follow our original intention and get round to Kinloch Hourn was out of the question and so after a bit of prospecting we decided on an ideal camp site almost on the beach of Barrisdale Bay. A nice stretch of level grass with bracken and fresh water laid on and a pebbly beach (without seaweed) on our doorstep. The view down the loch was grand and even though it seemed to be raining at different times either side of us we were rain free.

After soup, a 'fry', tea and things (preceded by a 'dip' in the sea) I had a 'do' at the Chronicles and then turned in around 10.30 after another appreciation of the setting of our camp.

MONDAY 30TH JULY

An early start this morning – 't would be 7.15 a.m.

The usual dip – a start on breakfast cooking and then the midges swung into action. The air was very still with plenty of fairly high cloud about (peaks not visible) – conditions which I suppose encourage low flying activities of this kind of craft. So we donned our nets – long trousers, pullover and managed to eat with a fair amount of comfort (we found however that the blighters *could* get thro' the net). Anyway a slight breeze helped things and after breakfast of porridge, a fry, toast & tea we broke camp about 9.30 – the tent much to Bob's relief, since he has to carry the thing, still dry.

The weather made a slight attempt at drizzle but didn't seem really keen on the idea and our walk along the shores of Loch Hourn to Kinloch Hourn was really delightful. The track being another really built up affair and the scenery all we could desire with many really fine examples of fully developed Scotch Pines. Definitely the finest stretch of the trek so far.

We made Kinloch Hourn about midday and decided to lunch at the farm belonging to E. MacRae who we learned took in visitors and had been rather busy this summer. Milk & four eggs were forthcoming but this time, the commercial side of things having reared its ugly head, we had to pay! The lunch was very good, the hardboiled egg which I had brought up from Manchester at last being brought into play. We also had date sandwiches & Ryvita.

After receiving advice as to the quickest and easiest way to Ratagan we skirted the head of Loch Beag and finally reached the Shooting Lodge – a well-kept place on the other side of the Loch. Here we asked for advice as to the whereabouts of the track to Coire Reidh (Ray). Young Donald the Gillie was summoned and proved very communicative telling us quite a few facts about this deer stalking business. Apparently the owner – a Major from Norfolk – is expected up in a month's time with his party. The importance of keeping the average weights of deer shot was also stressed – for that forest the average last year being 14 stones. The gillie seemed to think that women when they can shoot are more accurate than men!

After bidding farewell to the gillie we followed a well-made but steep path up the fir-clad hillside behind the lodge, eventually reaching without any trouble Coire Reidh. The clouds, especially to the South, were by this time lifting and on our way up we were rewarded by grand views of Loch Hourn and the mountains to the South. In view of the lifting cloud we decided to have a go for Sgurr na Sgine (3,098 ft).This was eventually reached after a sweat in sunshine but with terrific views either side.

In the interests of accuracy I think I ought to record this but please don't let it go any further. Halfway up Bob found a stream and suggested we get the Primus out and make a brew – unfortunately I was quite a distance off and had the Primus – so we didn't have a brew.

We made the top around 4 p.m. and the clouds were still high. We got a good view of the Saddle but couldn't see the Five Sisters of Kintail. (I was pleased to find I had climbed 2,000 ft. in 1¼ hrs. – ¼ hr. longer than usual for which credit is due to the heavy pack!)

We dropped down to Coire Chaoil in good time, seeing a herd of deer on the way, and selected a grand pool in a mtn. stream for a bathe and as a brewing spot. Bob agreed that with our goal almost in sight this was the right time of the day for the latter.

Following this very refreshing interlude we passed down a fairly decent track which together with the scenery improved as we approached the head of Loch Duich. We struck the road near the school and after a spot of repartee with some soldiers plodded up the road for another 20 or so minutes to reach Ratagan YH about 8.15 p.m.

Bob's parcel was awaiting him – loaves available and milk in any quantity from the farm.

The stove was rather crowded but Bob got cracking, whilst I went for the milk, and produced an excellent repast consisting of soup (from tin and not packet for a change) potatoes & sausages with the usual etcs. to follow. I seem to be fortunate in my cooks – it would seem that the qualification for any expedition in which I am involved must be 'can you cook and cook well?'!

The Warden proved to be a real Scot (Stuart kilt and all) with the usual Scottish droll sense of humour. 'The should be room on the bus for 1¾ of you.' – could Bob be the ¾?

TUESDAY 31ST JULY

Up bright (?) and early around 7.15 a.m. in order to be first on the stove. Two or three other early birds were about who assisted by fatherly guidance from Bob succeeded in lighting the stove.

Another milestone in the succession of successful meals was passed with a breakfast of porridge (with plenty milk), bacon & egg, toast & marmalade, tea.

Wrote 'Ratagan YH' cards to mother & M. and spent an hour or so writing up the Chronicles – general repartee with the Warden whilst this was in progress.

Left Hostel in dry weather cloud 1,500 to 2,000 ft. and tramped to village of Invershiel to post cards and check up on this 'ere bus to Kyle we had been told about. The Postmistress told us the bus left 8 a.m. and the next – well there wasn't one!

Met three lads from Hostel with complication of hooks and line who advised there was a pub ½ mile down the road actually selling beer. We didn't bother but made a mental note of same. They kindly sold me ten Capstan and promised to put us first on the list for any surplus fish.

From Shiel Bridge we tramped up the way we had come down the previous day but followed the main path to the right for a good way up the hillside to the Bealach before leaving same and strike across the hillside to meet a deer stalking path ready made to take us to the ridge. We had lunch at this point and noted that the cloud level was 2,000ish ft.

Soon we were in said cloud and passed with the aid of a compass over Sgurr Leac nan Each 3,013 ft., another 3,082 ft., Sgurr na Creige 3,196 ft.

Hereabouts the grassy ridge gave way to a more rocky affair with steep drops either side reminiscent of Crib Goch. All this time, except for some intriguing views through the cloud before Sgurr na Creige, we were in cloud and continued so until we were back on the 2,000 ft. mark at the end of the ridge.

Soon we were on the Saddle 3,317 ft. – a more complicated piece of ground with outcrops and ridges running out South-East and North.

With Bob assisting in the navigation we turned North by compass and managed to resist the usual temptation to take one of the more obvious ways and ignore the map. Heading due North in cloud we went up and down on an obvious ridge passing over a second peak called Sgurr na Creige 3,100 ft. to complete the fifth Munro for the day and the sixth of the expedition.

We were quickly below the cloud bank and reaching the end of the ridge we were rewarded with a magnificent panorama ahead and on either side. The peaks of the Five Sisters of Kintail were still in cloud and we couldn't see Skye but the rest stood out clear and well defined – Loch Duich looking particularly fine.

We shot down the hillside to find a 'gorgey' part of a stream where we bathed and crawled about up the rocky river bed to our hearts' content.

Back at Shiel Bridge for 6.05 p.m. (5 minutes later than schedule – terrible!) so we decided to walk round the ½ mile to the hotel for a drink. The ½ mile seemed more like a mile but was probably worth it. The bar room was well adorned with stag antlers taken from Kintail and surrounding forests.

Had a few words with an army officer, decided the barman had no idea of making shandies and returned to the trudge to the Hostel arriving at same about 7.15 p.m.

We had the cooking pretty well organised by this time and slammed a couple of pans of water on the stove as a sort of reservation whilst we changed.

Tonight we had 3½ pints of milk and an excellent dinner of potatoes, carrots, soup, toast, cake & chocolate supplied by stoutish Austrian young woman with the 'cosmopolitan' English intellectuals who would persist in taking my knife in mistake for one of their own.

The evening by this time was terrific – very little cloud, a golden (really) sunset in the West at the sea and of the Loch with the peaks of some of the Sisters and other mountains at the head of the Loch tinged rose pink.

Before turning in after the last time at this 'Camp 3' a word or two about the Hostel:

Has the best position on the Loch with marvellous views (weather permitting) – the most 'exposed privy' in Scotland, this is a brick structure with concrete roof all whitewashed and situated between the Hostel and the Loch. I fear Bob & I failed to show it due reverence for whilst 'waiting' this morning we decided the flat roof, which was about 8 ft. high, presented a nice sort of mantelshelf problem. The result was we spent most of the time on said roof to the amazement of the occupant.

A further climb of the 'gable end' variety was to be found on the barn at the end of the Hostel – one achieved the hay loft by a bit of finger work – not too difficult.

I like the sign on the door in letters of chromium – FAILTE – Gaelic for WELCOME.

The Hostel was opened about 1935 and I gathered that the present Warden was Warden then. Anyway he is a bright lad with a fine sense of humour. – 'From a distance the lavatory has often been mistaken for the castle.' 'I am going to have a glass door put in it because of the view.' After a warning that if we were up before seven we wouldn't get our cards we retired.

WEDNESDAY 1ST AUGUST

The rather tough looking middle-aged Scot who had come from Glen Affric with a 36 lb. pack (tent, blankets etc.) fishing for most of his food was about at 6.30 a.m. I was awake but lay low and in view of the sign on the Warden's door, 'BEWARE – INSIDE THIS DOOR THE WARDEN IS HIGHLY EXPLOSIVE' waited for the fun to begin. About 10 to 7 the door opened and downstairs shot the Warden in pyjamas. A short wordy dual ensued in which the Warden threatened to withhold the 'book' and back he returned to bed.

We were ready and downstairs by seven to find our 'books' propped up on the Warden's breakfast table. We got the Primus cracking and had a hurried breakfast of egg, bacon, tea bread & marmalade all in half an hour – for we had a bus to catch.

Bidding goodbye to the Warden who was up by this time we left 7.30 to do the 2 miles to Invershiel PO.

Clouds were low as we beat it along the road. The bus was due to leave 8 a.m. which means anything from 8 to 8.30, Scottish time, so I forged on ahead just in case.

Overtaking the Highlander just before Shiel Bridge I was treated to his opinion of the Warden who had made him wait until 7.20 or so before giving the Scot his 'book' – his accent was much Scottish and some words had to be guessed at by we Sassenachs.

The bus wasn't there of course and put in an appearance about 8.15 a.m. to collect the mail and a few other odds and ends including a furbished up stag antler and ourselves.

The journey around the Loch was full of interest even though the clouds were still low. The bus driver seemed to have a lot of commissions to carry out – parcels and letters being handed in at various points on the way with money and instructions as to how they were to be forwarded. Our bus driver also acted as postman – collected letters from pillar boxes as we went along. I expected any moment that a sheep or some such would be put on board but in this I was disappointed.

There was a halt made at the toll bridge which replaces the ferry at Dornie whilst the driver presumably went for breakfast. The bus got fuller and fuller but managed to take on all comers until we finally ran down to Kyle of Lochalsh in glorious sunshine.

Fortunately we had an hour and half to spare whilst we waited for the 11.35 train to Achnashellach. The time was used to replenish our supply of paraffin and meths, buy bread & kippers whilst I, on my part, refilled my pen at the PO, sent off a couple of cards, bought some cigs, had a 'cuppa' at MacDonald's Tea Rooms and generally wandered around Kyle. The scene was well worth seeing with Skye just across the way and the little ferry doing its stuff carrying cars (one a time) and folk between the island and the mainland.

We left rather reluctantly but the views from the train on our way up to Achnashellach were just perfect in the morning sunshine. During the journey we had lunch.

The Stationmaster at Achnashellach, who is also the Postmaster, had my parcel awaiting me and, except for a little damage to the chocolate during transit, all was in order. We left half the parcel for collection on our way back and were soon trudging up the path by the side of the River Lair.

The sky was cloudless but we reached Loch Coire Lair in good time. The setting of this loch was pretty fine with impressive craggy mountains, Sgorr Ruadh and Fuar Tholl to the SW and South and the ridge of Beinn Liath Mhor to the North, everything being flooded in sunshine.

We made a halt for an hour to bathe, sunbathe and have a brew – really enjoyable.

After this delightful interlude we continued up quite a good track to the pass between Sgorr Ruadh and Beinn Liath Mhor – a good narrow pass with Sgorr Ruadh making an impressive background. This mountain has some features very similar to Pillar and its shape and appearance suggest that it might provide good rock climbing.

We dropped down a steep portion and soon after this left the path to branch right towards Lochan Neimhe. This didn't look too inviting for a camp site so we carried on West down the side of the stream through rough going moraine country (there are excellent evidences of glacier action on the sides of the mountains above the moraine). Immediately we had a good view of Loch Torridon we pitched camp 4 by the side of the stream.

The surrounding peaks on the way down could all be clearly seen and were a delight, the ridge of Beinn Liathach with its 'pinkles' looking especially fine – this being on the agenda for the morrow.

The supper will go down in history because of the sunset over the Loch on the one hand and an attack of midges very much on the other.

The midge attack started about the end of the soup course. We managed to get through the meal somehow by skilful manipulation of our 'veils' but afterwards even though wearing long trousers, hats with nets, pullovers etc. we were still very much troubled.

I finished up sat in the middle of the stream dipping my hands in the water, soaking my face every few minutes and smoking furiously. This seemed to have a measure of success as apart from the ease given to the existing bites, I noticed that the only midge which alighted on my wrist was drowned! Thank goodness no photographer was present!

We turned in about 10.30.

THURSDAY 2ND AUGUST

All the tops were in cloud when we started in on breakfast 7.30ish. We had for breakfast porridge with dried milk, dried egg omelette & bacon, tea & marmalade after which I did a spot of Chronicles writing.

After packing my rucksack with just the day's necessities we set a course up stream (leaving camp about 10.45) for Lochan Neimhe and then down the other side to reach the road below the Eastern end of Liathach about noon. A pause was made at this point and then we commenced the long grind up the foothills followed by what must be the steepest and longest heather covered slope I, at least, have experienced.

We stopped for lunch at a marvellous viewpoint around the 2,000 ft. mark just below cloud level and overlooking the coire between Beinns Eighe and Liathach with mountains to the NW visible. I was also intrigued to find that the farthermost loch I could see to the SE was called Loch Coulin (shades of Skye!)

There was a fine track not shown on the map in the coire below. Being on the NE corner of the mountain we also began to appreciate the steepness of the North side of Liathach.

Leaving this grand spot about 2.15 we were soon in cloud and climbing steadily over numerous sharply cut stones and boulders – the first likeness to the 'Coolin' Ridge. Hereabouts I noticed the first evidences of a party going in our direction – triconni marks in moss and scratch marks on the rocks – presumably a party which had taken advantage of the fine clear weather yesterday.

We quickly met a decent sized cairn but as later events proved this was not the peak of the first 3,000 footer of the ridge but probably served to mark the end of the ridge. Dropping down and then climbing much higher up a very steep portion (hereabouts a rabbit got up) over rocks we reached the first named summit – Stuc a Choire Dhuibh Bhig 3,050 ft. – what a name!

The ridge was very narrow, with grand steep falls on the Northern side, and after a few false alarms, as we were all this time in cloud, we finally gained the summit of the central and highest peak – Spidean a'Choire Leith 3,456 ft. – the highest of our expedition so far.

The ridge became really interesting after this for we began to meet the pinkles. Talk about inefficiency up and down, up and down! – but what a glorious ridge. Especially did we appreciate this when dropping a little lower we could see the road below on the South side and Loch Coire na Caime on the North side.

We noticed that the nail scratches followed the same direction as we were taking and, without flattering ourselves unduly, it struck us that some members of the party at least must be rock climbers.

The pinkles gave way to a smooth ridge falling precipitously on the North side and more gradually on the South. Except for one or two minor peaks the ridge now led easily up to the last Munro – Mullach an Rathain 3,358 ft. – it was now about 5.30. (The ninth of our trip, and last).

We descended a short way due West and then changed direction SW to strike the head of a very much rock strewn and steep gully. Dropping down below cloud level we were pleased to note that we were in the gully we had decided on yesterday as a direct means of descent to Loch Torridon. More pleasing still was the scene before our eyes – most of Loch Torridon, the mountains to the SW and the Northern end of Skye lay before us like a map, with the sun gleaming on the sea.

We set course for the NE end of the Loch where there seemed a goodly number of houses and crofts. Just before reaching the road we met a man with a sheep dog who was apparently going just a little further up the hillside to gather a newly cut fleece.

A halt was made for the usual chat during which we enquired where we could *buy* eggs & milk – we inserted 'buy' deliberately because by this time we were becoming rather embarrassed at the repeated gifts of these things.

He thought we would have little trouble and added 'are you down from the Hills' – 'yes'. 'Then you must come and have tea', – we accepted with thanks. The house was nearby and what a house! – We expected a simple cottage and found a stone built detached affair with bay windows and well-furnished including a fine bathroom containing porcelain fittings.

Our newly found friend told his wife to make tea. Soon cups appeared, but this was not all, other things appeared also until finally we sat down to a full table loaded with oatcakes, scones, cheese, crowdie, pats of butter, jam & cake.

We stayed 2 hrs. or so talking solidly, during which we managed to 'sell' hydro-electricity power generation and learned quite a few things. Our friend was not a shepherd as we had supposed but worked on the roads and ran a croft (few sheep, cow, crops, bees, turkeys being fed on hard boiled eggs etc.) as a sideline. He turned out to be a good example of an intelligent Scot, many of whom have had a secondary school education. Both Bob & I learned of a new one re. Harris tweeds – apparently there are four colours of wool naturally coloured as grown on the sheep i.e. white, grey, black and light brown – the last mentioned being peculiar to Harris sheep which are very small and are hand plucked.

Another thing was that the grouse have left or are pretty scarce in Scotland these days – certainly we couldn't recollect hearing the cry of this bird during our travels. Midges – the wife seemed to think that talcum powder (or face powder) was a good protection against their activities. Our road mender put his faith in a piece of muslin in which two holes were cut for seeing. He seemed to think that midges had not been too bad this year!

At last we rose to make our departure, whereupon we were *presented* with a billy can full of fine milk & a dozen eggs. Bob promised to loan our friend his copy of *I Bought a Mountain* by Firbanks because it was clear that both the man and his wife read a lot – especially during the long winter nights which the wife preferred.

We 'gently' walked up the valley in the gathering dusk to our camp – noting on the way a good sized waterfall which could supply quite a number of kW of hydro-electricity.

A good soup (one of Bob's specialities) and a 'cuppa' were consumed and after admiring another fine sunset we turned in around 11 p.m.

Friday 3rd August

7.30 a.m. was the time we managed to part with our sleeping bags which, all week, alone had been plenty warm enough. Cloud was well down and a slight drizzle fell intermittently but this didn't stop us from continuing the uninterrupted run (excepting the midge episodes) of meals cooked and eaten outside the tent.

We did ourselves well this a.m. – porridge with of course our super milk followed by eggs (two of 'em each) & bacon, toast, tea.

I did some writing, then we packed the tent, cleared up the site, and pushed our way up the hillside due South around 11 a.m., making an easy beeline for the track from Torridon to Coulag in Glen Carron.

Slight drizzle was in evidence but we soon struck the path – just after an aged man had passed going down to Torridon – from whence he came I do not know for it was still earlish.

The track was, as usual, very well made and we hadn't the slightest difficulty, even though in mist at the higher levels, in finding our way. This led around the Northern shore of Loch an Eoin, thence over the col between Maol Chean-dearg and Meall Dearg down to Loch Coire Fionnaraich where a halt was made for lunch around 1.30.

The Loch was delightful complete with sandy shore and strip jutting out into deep water – so we swam!

The centre of attraction of our lunch was hard boiled eggs – seven of which had been so treated after breakfast this a.m.

We continued on leisurely down the valley and soon I realised the ambition of my journey (which incidentally came to life in the pub at Invershiel) – I obtained an antler or at least the offside portion of one. According to Bob – the owner of same in making a savage charge at my person became entangled with my beard – to Bob's secret delight I fear, my facial appearance having weighed heavily on his mind for many a day – apparently it lowered the tone of the party! To continue – during the ensuing struggle, which was awful to behold and lasted for 1 hour 31 mins. 25 secs. approximately, one antler must have lost its grip. Anyway the struggle terminated with same snapping off at the root, thus releasing the stag which departed for higher altitudes to forever shun the paths of man.

After this sidelight we continued on our downward trek passing the time of the day with a NZ pilot and youth on the way up for the fishing (the Hooker falls are apparently very wide!)

Hitting the road above Coulags we plodded up the road the 3 or 4 miles to Achnashellach where we found a spot on the waterfall in the R. Lair for tea.

Changes were effected after which, looking a little more civilised, we caught the 6.05 p.m. train to Inverness. During the journey I completed Bob's happiness by shaving – not without some trepidation as the one and only blade began to lose its edge with only one side of my face done – fortunately I made it!

During a longish halt at Achnasheen I learned this was one of the worst spots for midges – the theory being that it was due to the heather; there certainly was a lot around.

At Inverness, together with a naval officer returning from Skye (a good lad) we decided to catch the 11.20 p.m. train to Perth, which we made about 5 a.m. and promptly got the Primus going on the station to heat some cold tea brought down from Inverness.

Our ways parted at this juncture, I to continue down to Edinburgh on the 6.50 a.m. train and Bob to London on a later train.

And so, still clutching our tent poles, we journeyed out of the best cross country mountaineering expedition both Bob & I have experienced – there should have been the sound of bagpipes in the distance and a sunset hereabouts but the stage manager overslept!

ALEX AND HARRY ON BEINN FHADA, ROSS AND CROMARTY EASTER 1944.

A LAMENT

Come, mourn the loss of Harry's hat.
The perfect hat. Old as the hills.
Weathered by time and nature's moods,
Caressed by the breeze and the sun's hot kiss
Until it reached perfection.

Oh, it was such a famous hat!
A lovely hat. Known on the hills.
Scaling the peaks and craggy heights.
Tramping the moors and leafy lanes.
Resting in pubs and in the draughty tent.
It was indeed perfection.

Oh mourn the loss of Harry's hat.
That super hat perfect the fit,
Until the wind in jealous rage,
Snatched at its brim with fingers cruel.
Then tossed on the sea, in proud distain,
It met the great unknown.

Margot H. Parker (Mitchell)
Llandudno, 20 February 1946.